STOP ACTING
START LIVING

BERNARD HILLER

Cover Picture - Marcin Lobaczewski taken in Lodz, Poland
Back Picture - Jordan Engle taken in Los Angeles, USA.
Graphic Designer - Adrian Gaeta

First published by Dog Ear Publishing
4010 W. 86th Street, Ste H
Indianapolis, IN 46268
www.dogearpublishing.net

dog ear
PUBLISHING

ISBN: 978-1-4575-1735-8

This book is printed on acid-free paper.

Printed in the United States of America

My Parents Dora and Jose Hiller

Dedication

This book is dedicated to all the teachers around the world who make a difference. I believe that being a teacher is the most noble and important profession. Where would you be if you didn't have a teacher in your life?

I would like to thank all my teachers and mentors that I have met along the way. I especially want to thank my first two teachers, my wonderful parents, Dora and Jose Hiller who taught me to love life and to make a difference in this world. They made me believe that I could do anything and that everything was possible. They were Holocaust survivors and even though they lost most of the members of their families they gave me all the joy and love I ever wanted. They were both lovers of the Yiddish Theatre and it was there that I first encountered the magic of performing. There was lots of singing, dancing and humor. I was so intrigued by how transformed audiences were once they left the theatre. I'm grateful to them for introducing me to such an amazing profession. I also want to thank my wonderful brother Jaime and my beautiful sister Golda for always standing by me and cheering me on. And to all my wonderful extended family in Los Angeles and in New York, I really appreciate your love and support.

This book was encouraged by my family and actor friends who always said, "When are you going to write your book?" Well, here it is! A Special thank you to Winnie who encouraged me to teach and to my incredibly talented children Dora and David who made me become a better person. I love you. Also massive thanks to all the great acting teachers who have come before me, some that I have met and some whose books I have read. You have influenced my perception of what is possible. Thank you to my writing partner Kevin Hutchings, for your energy and the great ideas that made this book happen. It was a real pleasure working with you. And a special thanks to my copywriters Adrian Gaeta and Rachel Hiller. Read this book and become the artist and person you were born to be & remember... ***"The Bigger The Dream The Better The Life"***.

Al Pacino told my Masterclass
"I'm always open to learn!"

CONTENTS

Foreword by Brett Ratner

"Four years ago Bernard Hiller called my office and invited me to speak at his Masterclass, but due to my busy schedule I was unable to do so. Eventually I got another call and it just so happened that I was free, and my instinct was telling me I should go.

When I entered his studio I was overwhelmed by such a positive energy and enthusiasm. I was thinking, "What is going on here?" I had never felt this kind of energy at any other acting class before. These actors were open, happy and seemed hungry to learn. I planned to only stay for an hour, but found myself not wanting to leave. I was so impressed with the level of the work that I invited the actors to my home to show them a documentary I had produced about the late great actor John Cazale. This was the start of my working relationship with Bernie, which I now call him. He was the only acting teacher I had met who could pinpoint in minutes, an actor's block and help them find a path in fulfilling their artistic dream.

It was a special gift to witness.

I now make it a point to attend his classes whenever I can. I even traveled to Paris once to meet some of his French actors. It was amazing to me to discover that he teaches all over the world. When I go to his classes not only do I learn, but I have also met some of the most wonderful and talented people. Bernie always says, "Happy people discover more talent". Over the years I have been able to use some of the actors I have met in his classes.

Everyone's artistic journey is different, but you will need guides and mentors along the way to succeed. I have had many throughout my career. I know that Bernie's book will help you change the way you look at your career and your life. It will show you how to reach your potential and be successful in this business. Remember you will have to apply the information you are given to achieve your dreams. So what are you waiting for? This book will help you discover the path to your success and live the life you've always wanted.

—Brett Ratner
Director "X-Men", "Rush Hour".

**Brett Ratner & Casting Director April Webster
at the opening of our showcase.**

"The book is a revelation. I have seen firsthand what happens to actors when they are given the tools to eliminate self-sabotage and to celebrate their most vital, vibrant selves. With incredible insight Bernard helps the actors see their gifts and helps them know, many for the first time, that they have the ability and freedom to be as creative and successful as they can be."

—**April Webster**
*Casting Director – "Lost", "Star Trek",
"Mission Impossible 3 & 4", and "Super 8".*

BEING AN ARTIST
IS NOT A CHOICE

I'm on stage. Age 3.

I was inspired to become an actor when I was very young, but it was the story I heard when I was six years old, from a man from Salonika, Greece, that showed me the power of acting.

He told me that when he was young, the Nazis occupied Greece, and rounded up all the Jews in Salonika. As he was running for his life, soldiers rounded a corner and spotted him in the middle of the street. The soldiers saw him and he saw them. He didn't know what to do or where to go, because there was nowhere to hide.

As they came closer to him, in an instant, he contorted every part of his body into the state of a physically and mentally challenged person. He walked with jerky movements and spoke as if he had a major speech impediment. As one of the soldiers went to grab him for

1

deportation, another said, "Oh forget him, he's not even human". They left him behind and moved on to others.

It was amazing to me to hear about this man's transformation. As the Nazi soldiers were looking right at him, he let his instinct take over and became someone else. This man was not an actor. He didn't have a second take. He couldn't say, "Oh, can I try this again?" At that moment, he realized that there was no other choice.

"Acting saved his life."

When someone comes up to me and asks if they should be an actor I tell them, "Acting is not a choice, you don't choose it, it chooses you". It is in your DNA. You become an actor not because you want to, but because you have to. Why would anyone choose acting? It's a difficult profession with constant rejection and a life of uncertainty. Totally Crazy!

You do it because you know deep inside, that this is what you were born to do. Now, if you come into this business wanting to find fame you will fail, but if you love the craft, you will work. Remember, success is what you give yourself and fame is what others give you.

True artists never need motivation to train or to take steps that will bring them closer to their goals. They will do whatever it takes, because they have an artistic need that is on fire. It is something they are working on everyday and they're not waiting for anyone to give them permission to create. If anyone or anything can stop you from being an artist then it's not the career for you.

Acting is one of the most wonderful professions in the world. If you're fortunate enough to be born to act, consider yourself lucky. Acting is also very important to society, because it teaches the world how to live and how to connect to one another. Through films and plays we become aware of our commonalities.

If acting is what you really want to do, then you must learn to enjoy the process. It's the journey and the people you meet along the way that will be the most gratifying part of being an artist.

"Acting is not a choice, you don't choose it, it chooses you."

THE LANGUAGE OF SUCCESS

Art is a reflection of life and there is nothing more important than understanding the mechanisms of our lives. When we fail in that, we fail creatively and personally. To understand acting you must comprehend the intricacies of life. I've come to understand that to succeed in acting you need to succeed in life. The greater your understanding of life, the more successful you will be.

I have been in this business for 35 years and I teach people everywhere how to become stars in their own lives, relationships and in their careers.

I also want actors to create their own opportunities and so I teach what I call, *"The Language of Success"*. Most acting schools consider teaching the business of show-business as not "artistic" and give the actors the feeling that by choosing to follow their dream, they will just live a life of suffering. Well, that is just a myth. I help actors around the world accomplish their goals and live their lives with passion.

When I first started teaching I read a quote from the great acting teacher Uta Hagen. A light bulb went on over my head and triggered me to develop a new approach to acting. She said, "Acting is the worst taught subject on the planet". I felt that she was right. Actors were not being given the tools needed in the development of their talent and even more, not being taught the business of *Show-Business*. When actors have talent but are unable to use it, their dreams soon turn into nightmares.

The art of acting is constantly evolving, but acting training has been taught in very much the same fashion for years. Without learning newer techniques you will be left behind. Nobody wants to see people act anymore. They want to see the actor become the part. All the great performances of our time happen when the actor disappears on the screen and you only see the character.

The techniques listed in this book will bring you to that state of being, but technique is not enough anymore. Life coaching, personal development and business training are now very important key elements in creating a *successful* artist. I have developed techniques, which bring them together in a profound new way.

"Success is a lifestyle."

I feel that many books just give you a temporary route to achieving dreams. This book is meant to teach you a way of life because "Success is not an accident, success is a lifestyle". This book helps you discover and fix "**why**" you haven't succeeded yet and the underlining issues that are stopping you.

Every one of us is born with a special gift, but we must discover, nurture and develop it, for it to appear in our lives. You must locate the treasures inside you to realize your full potential. It's time for you to wake up to the true brilliant, creative, loving and powerful self, which is hidden underneath your "stories" and negative belief systems. Motivation only lasts a week, fixing the real problems that are stopping you can last a lifetime.

"Would you win an Oscar for the way you live your life?"

Greatness is not something that only the lucky few are destined to achieve. Greatness is a choice. It is something we are all capable of. We have been put on this earth with limitless potential. We can leave a mark on this world only when we realize our own self worth. These techniques will give you a way to facilitate a great performance on stage and in your life. By understanding human psychology and the dynamics of success, these techniques might even win you an Academy Award. I often ask people, "Would you win an Oscar for the way you live your life?"

Well, I'm here to teach you how to do that. I currently teach actors and business people in various countries, many of whom come to Los Angeles to continue training with me. These techniques have the ability to change the lives of everyday people, but also help very established actors and top business people take their careers and lives to the next level.

I started my own artistic journey at The High School of Performing Arts in New York City. The "Fame School". It was there that I started training to become an actor, singer and dancer. After becoming a performer I toured the US with many Broadway musicals and performed in opera houses throughout Europe. I also did plays in New York and L.A. and have appeared in over 200 TV commercials. I have guest-starred on several television shows and appeared in numerous films. I am currently producing several major motion pictures, one of which I wrote based on the story of "Brundibar".

I started my teaching career in New York City, when I was asked by an actor to help him get a part in a Broadway show. He booked the role that changed his career and after that, more actors asked me to coach them. The actors I coached became successful and eventually I was teaching classes.

I then started to work with many people in the business world such as Swarovski Crystal. I was called to stimulate the creative process and help them to invent new product ideas. Since then, I have been fortunate to work with Nadja Swarovski and her team. Together we have taken the company principals to another level. It's a pleasure to work with business people who are looking to learn and grow.

Soon, other major companies asked me to work with their sales teams. I was applying my "acting" techniques to teach them how to creatively solve problems and become powerful speakers and presenters. When financial companies meet prospective clients, they only have 20 minutes to give their message and convince them to give millions of dollars to invest and manage. They needed an edge; they needed a different approach to succeed against the competition. It was extremely rewarding to see these techniques succeed with business people.

When I relocated to Los Angeles in 1990, I started to work with some very successful actors and others who wanted to be successful. One of my first clients was a model who had never acted before. She was 21 and very beautiful, but lacked confidence in the acting process. She was a bit scared and nervous as she was going in to audition for a tiny role in a film called *The Mask*, with Jim Carrey. Her name was Cameron Diaz. She had never acted before and of course felt a bit lost, so I proceeded to teach her exactly what to do at her audition. I could see that she was very eager to learn and follow instructions. She did so well at her first audition that they asked her to read for the leading role of the film. The leading role of a major feature film, wow!

We now needed to dig in and reach a whole new level of her abilities quickly. When she entered my studio and told me what had happened she was a bit shocked and didn't know exactly what all that entailed. I told her not to worry and that she would be ready for her next challenge.

Over the next few weeks we worked on her auditions. She read for that part over 13 times. Casting an unknown actress in a major motion picture is a very risky proposition. Finally, she called me with the news that she had landed the part of a lifetime. I am proud to say, that audition launched her incredible film career. Through the work we did, she believed that she already had the job when she walked into the room. She was the person they were looking for. I'm still very proud of how she has handled her incredible success.

Another actor I worked with is Chace Crawford, now the star of the hit series *Gossip Girl*. When we started, he was disconnected from his power. As we worked on finding his blocks to his true feelings, we also found old negative messages that were stopping him from reaching his full potential. One day a casting director, Denise Chamian, who had just worked for Steven Spielberg, came to see my class and spotted Chace. She said he had the "it" factor. We had worked very hard to find and display this "it" factor to the world. That started his whole career. There are times in your life when you must seize your moment, and in this case Chace was now ready.

"Thank you Bernard for teaching a man like me that it was okay to cry and for allowing me to face my demons and feel again."

—Emilio Rivera
Actor - *Traffic, Sons of Anarchy*

Emilio Rivera is the exception to every rule. I met Emilio when I went to give a one hour lecture at a school, on how to succeed as an artist. As it turned out, it was a school in a 'rough and tough' neighborhood. When I finished my lecture, I quickly headed out the door. Suddenly this huge man looking like a gang member came up to me and said in a heavy accent, "Do you teach privately?" Which I do, but I told him that I was totally full, which was not exactly true. I thought, I couldn't teach him. As I walked away I heard a voice inside me say, "If anyone could help this guy, it could be you". I turned back to him and said, "Okay, I'll work with you". For the next two years I had to train him about the basics of life. And I mean the real fundamentals of life. He had no father. He was married, but spent most of his time with his gang. He was living in the underworld of gang life and I had to teach him how to live in real society. He didn't quite understand anything about relationships, ethics or life. One day he started to cry. Letting his emotions out changed everything. This was a huge step for him, because that would never be allowed in the world in which he grew up.

He told me that I was the only person who he was ever afraid of because I had the courage to tell him the truth. After two years of this basic life work I started to teach him about how to become a great actor and the language of success. Of all the people I have ever worked with, no one will ever impress me more than Emilio. He went from a gang member living in constant fear of death, to an extremely successful actor and moral human being. Since then, he has worked with Tom Cruise, George Clooney, Julia Roberts, Jim Carrey and many more. He was in the Oscar winning film *Traffic*, has a leading role on *Sons of Anarchy* and they are developing a TV show based on his life story. Wow! He is the ultimate success story. When I think of him, it makes me smile.

LL Cool J recently came to me, after working years in the industry, because he wanted to get better as an actor. He is currently on the hit

TV show *NCIS: Los Angeles*. LL Cool J already has had an amazing career and yet he is always hungry to learn. That's a true star.

These artists and many others have had incredible breakthroughs. In Hollywood, I'm known as the "Doctor". They say, "Go see Bernard, he will figure out what is *really* stopping you". As Einstein once said, "The person, who creates the problem, cannot solve the problem". You will need someone outside yourself to figure out what's wrong.

Talent is not the most important ingredient to being successful here in Hollywood. You must have an unstoppable desire to succeed and do something every day that brings you closer to your dream. A dream without goals or deadlines is just a dream that will never become reality. An effective business plan teaches you how to create a career that can last a lifetime. I feel that this book will not only benefit every person who reads it, but also hopefully encourage you to change the world in some profound and lasting way.

"I just wanted to tell you, that your work is much more important than acting itself.

It's much more important than being a singer.

Much more than being a dancer, much more than doing movies.

Without people like you, there wouldn't be any stars.

Without teachers like you, actors are nothing.

Without artists like you,

Art is nothing."

—**Milad Klein**
Actor, Germany

BEFORE YOU BEGIN
FIRST THINGS FIRST

For years, I had studied with many of the most respected acting teachers in New York City, but it was only after I read Eric Morris' book, "No Acting Please", that I realized that the 15 years of so called "great" training I had gotten, wasn't going to work. Not because the classes weren't any good, but because the acting training I was being taught was totally out of order and missing some important key elements.

There was one phrase in Eric's book that hit me in a very profound way, "Acting is a living problem". At first I didn't quite understand what he meant. It took me a while to grasp the true meaning of this phrase, but once I did, it changed my life and my understanding of acting forever. I realized that I needed to change my life to change my career. I also started to feel that acting teachers were not dealing with the fundamental problems that are responsible for why so many actors are not successful. I recognized that the most under taught topics are how to achieve success once you are getting the training you need, and how to rid yourself of the personal blocks and fears that are stopping you from truly connecting to your talent. There are hundreds of thousands of people studying acting all over the United States and around the world every day, but there are very few success stories. Why? I noticed that some of the best waiters came out of the finest acting schools in New York City. They pay $40,000 a year to go to a school that wasn't teaching them how to be successful. They studied the craft, but not how to succeed in Show- Business. Something was not right.

I also realized that my own lack of acting success at that time came from being disconnected from myself and not knowing enough about who I really was inside. I was not open or grateful enough, and I did not really trust my instincts. Once I started to recognize these issues in myself, I was able to see them in so many of the actors I was studying with. I was able to see how the lack of support they had experienced throughout their childhood and life had made them angry, sad and lonely, in pain and generally disconnected from themselves and others. No one seemed to be speaking about this in a powerful or meaningful way. These problems were the real reasons I thought students were not progressing as artists. I knew that if I would ever start to teach, I would take this type of training even further and deeper than ever before. After doing this type of work for so many years, I feel that all artists should train like this in the future.

Before you begin this incredible journey, you must know that all actors go through 4 stages of learning.

Stage 1: Unconscious Incompetence

If you are at this level, you are not aware of how disconnected, unskilled and unprepared you are for this journey. Everyone who enters Show-Business always has blocks and fears that they need to overcome, but at this level you are not even aware what they are.

Stage 2: Conscious Incompetence

At this stage you become fully aware of what your artistic and personal limitations and weaknesses are, but are not sure how to overcome them. There will be moments when you feel that you will never be able to prevail over all your blocks and fears. Embrace this feeling and know that this is all part of the process.

Stage 3: Conscious Competence

You reach this level only after you have trained a lot and are aware of what you have to do to perform successfully. But, it has not yet become second nature to you. If you don't think about it, it won't happen. For example, it is like your first time driving. You have to be fully conscious of what you have to do, to safely reach your destination.

Stage 4: Unconscious Competence

At this stage you are performing at the highest level of an artist without any thinking at all. It has become second nature to you. You are operating from your instinct and heart. At this final level you are experiencing the joy and freedom of being an artist.

"When I met Bernard Hiller for the first time, I was pretty shocked. He is very straightforward. He is so passionate about acting and actors. He sees what specific things you need to work on as an artist, but also as a human being right away, and that's the key to everything! His classes are breathtaking, revolutionary and life changing. In my opinion Bernard Hiller is the most original Acting Coach working today."

Ramin Dustar,
Austrian – Actor

THE ACTING CONTRACT

Whenever students come to see me they are always interested in telling me what they would like to get from me. What they would like me to teach them or what they didn't like from other teachers they have worked with. Some are very clear about what they want to learn and others are not sure. I have realized that for this learning process to be successful, it can't be a one-way street. It's not only what you want from your teacher, but also what your teacher wants from you.

I came up with a contract, which states exactly what I need from each student. It is true that finding a great teacher is difficult, but finding a great student is also difficult. If you're not a great student you will not be successful in the class, even if you're with a brilliant teacher. I found that most students are unaware *how* to really learn, which is why I wrote this contract. Below are specific rules and regulations, which if you abide by, we will both be successful in this endeavor.

The Acting Contract.

(A contract is an agreement between two parties clearly stating what is required.)

1. **I must have the courage to find the real "truth" about myself.**
   (Most people have no idea who they "truly" are. It's a very big problem.)

2. **I understand that to achieve my dreams, I must be willing to feel foolish and be uncomfortable.**
   (Are you ready to leave your comfort zones?)

3. **When I perform I will give more than anyone ever expected. Including myself.**
   (You need to constantly prove to yourself that you are serious about your dream.)

4. **I know that I will meet people who will not see my gift.**
   (That is the most common thing in the world, but it must never stop you.)

5. **I will not judge my gift. I will let others do that.**
    (Your job is just to give your gift to the world without any kind of judgment.)

6. **I am totally responsible for my career and myself.**
    (Accept where you are in your career, if you don't like it, only *you* can change it.)

7. **I will be very easy to work with.**
    (You'd be surprised how many difficult people try to get into this business, and of course fail. So, be very nice!)

8. **I will never complain or blame anyone.**
    (When you complain or blame anyone you lose your power.)

9. **I will be open to new information and new possibilities.**
    (Forget what you think you know and be open to what you didn't know.)

10. **I will bring more passion and joy to my craft, every day.**
    (Without passion and joy, your dream will just stay an idea.)

11. **I must be optimistic, especially during the tough times.**
(The secret of all successful people is that they are optimistic when others would not be.)

12. **I will learn to trust and believe in my artistic instincts.**
(Don't question your instincts they come from your heart - they're always right.)

13. **I understand that to achieve all of this, I must first-WAKE UP!!!**
(You may not know it, but trust me, you are sleeping. Wake up to your possibilities!)

I know that I will have to remind myself of all the above items daily.

I am totally committed to becoming a world-class artist and I agree with the above contract without question or reservation.

_____ Date_____4/21/17_____

WHAT DO YOU BRING TO SHOW BUSINESS THAT WE DON'T ALREADY HAVE?

"That's a very interesting question", most actors tell me.

Well it also happens to be the most important question you need to answer before you begin your acting journey. Most people have absolutely no idea how to answer that question and don't seem to know who they are or what is unique or special about them. Do you know what's unique or special about you?

This industry is not called Show-Up or Show-Off, but Show-**Business**. In a business you have to be very clear about what your product is. What do you have to offer that an audience might want to buy?

The answer to that is always, **YOU**. We don't have you. You are one of a kind. But just to be clear, I'm not speaking about the way you might be right now. I am speaking about a fully authentic and fully alive you. There is a huge difference. To become that, you'll need to be fully aware in all aspects of your life. That's where this journey begins. For example, you need to be in healthy and positive relationships. You need to go to museums, operas, ballets, plays and movies. Learn new topics, travel the world and connect with people from all walks of life. This will make you a dynamic person. If you are not fully engaged in life you are likely to be boring or a person without any passion, and no one is going to want to work with you. Dynamic people make dynamic artists and sad people make sad artists. Who would you like to work with? If you're sad, angry, lost or depressed, that's not the real you. It just means that you have unresolved personal issues that are holding you back. You must work through those issues immediately. The moment you crash through those roadblocks you will find the authentic you and become powerful beyond measure. You will need a mentor to help you with this.

You also need to know that in the beginning of your career you will be hired for acting jobs based on how you look. So ask yourself, "What parts will I be asked to play based on my appearance?" If you look sexy or funny can you comfortably and brilliantly access those parts of yourself? You might have to work on your appearance. I find that most students don't have a clear picture of themselves and need some professional advice on this very important topic. Once you answer these questions, you then have to learn how to play these parts in your unique way. There is no one who can play a part the way you play it when you're being your "authentic self". Realize, that if you see things differently then you must bring those differences into your auditions and your work. It's good that you don't see the part the way other people see it, because then you are making your own unique choices.

Finding an artistic family is also an important ingredient to your success. Unlike other professions, acting requires group energy to succeed. You must be around teachers that encourage your differences and support your unique qualities. Many great artists were often criticized or even ostracized when they first began, because they were considered to be "too different". Herein lies a central issue. Most people want to be liked so badly that they will never become their true selves. They are too afraid to be distinct from those around them. They don't want to stick out. Questions like "Why can't you be like everybody else?" and "Who do you think you are?" start to affect your behavior. If your main goal in life is to be liked by others, then you can never become authentic and you will fail in achieving your dream.

When you think of the great stars of the present or even long ago, you think about them because they are unique and aren't afraid to be their exclusive, irreplaceable selves. Actors like Marlon Brando, Marilyn Monroe, James Dean, Meryl Streep and Johnny Depp, knew who they were and never held back. They took risks and showed us their magnificent selves. That is what you will need to do. The great Russian acting teacher Stanislavski once said, "We don't need another actor who is like someone we already have". You are a once in a lifetime creation. So, give your unique gift to the world and you will be noticed. Don't copy someone else, because nothing is as good as the original.

Remember: Show the world something they haven't quite seen before. The unique and authentic **YOU**!

**Getting ready with the actors for our showcase with
Co-Director April Webster.**

WHAT ARE YOU SELLING?

W hen you walk through any famous shopping district in any great city, such as Rodeo Drive in Beverly Hills, there are many amazing stores that all have one thing in common; they all want you to walk in and ultimately buy something. Whether you enter or not will be based on your needs and the store's quality, appearance and atmosphere.

Think of yourself as a store. For discussion purposes let's call you "The President" of your store. As The President you are in charge of your store's success. So, if customers are not coming into your store then the blame is yours alone. A store without customers will quickly go out of business.

Do you have customers who are interested in you? Who want to know what you're selling? Do you have a personality; energy, charisma and a positivity that makes people want to get to know you? If the answer is no, then you must immediately start working on yourself. All of us, but especially artists, need people to come into our store to find out what we're selling, particularly since you are standing next to another "store" that is also trying to get their attention.

Potential customers (like casting directors, agents, producers and directors) do not have time to go into every store. They have to be very selective, and will only go into a store that they feel has everything they are seeking. Michael Levine, a Hollywood publicist once said in my class, "It's not who you know in this business, it's who would want to know you". If you are closed off, sad, or angry, you won't attract any customers. It doesn't matter what you're selling, no one will want to buy from you.

Since there is such strong competition out there, you have to be incredibly open and incredibly welcoming to succeed. Start by looking at yourself. Do people come up to you and wonder, "Who are you?" If the answer is "no" then you have a crisis on your hands. You might feel that your front door is open for business, but to others standing outside, it appears closed. Without a great "open door policy", you will fail, no matter how good the product is inside.

You need to be able to look at yourself in the mirror and see the outside first. How do you look? (You may need professional help with that; self-assessment rarely works). Are you aware of your "type" and are you marketing yourself in the appropriate way? Industry professionals first judge your outward appearance and find where you will fit in the marketplace. Then they read what your energy is. Within the first moment you walk into a room, they know what you are thinking and what you are feeling. Hollywood runs on energy and you have to find out what type of energy you are putting out there. Ask yourself this question: From all the stores out there would you go into your own store first?

Let's say that for a store to operate successfully it needs 10 departments to run it. I want you to imagine that you have 10 departments inside you working on your behalf. You, as The President of the company, have to inspire each department to perform at its very best. If your employees show up to work and see that you, The President, are depressed or lacking energy and vision, they will get very disheartened and become less productive. They won't work as hard, because they know that there is no future in this company. In fact, some of them will wish they could work at another company. To have a successful business you have to motivate your employees. You have to inspire them. Are you doing that? Are you willing to make all the necessary changes needed to achieve success?

As you look through your 10 departments, you will find that some are not as strong as others. Understand that all of the departments have to be working together, in sync. If they aren't working that way, it is because you haven't shown all the departments how to operate efficiently, and you're lacking the necessary leadership qualities. You will need to learn how to do that.

HERE ARE THE TEN DEPARTMENTS THAT MAKE UP YOUR STORE:

Department One: The Department of Problem Solving.

There will always be problems in a business, that is a given. If you can't solve your problems creatively, your company is going to close.

Remember: obstacles are a sign of life and any dream or goal you pursue will present obstacles. *The bigger the dream; the bigger the obstacles.* You need a strong department that focuses on problem *solving* so that you can deal with any issues quickly and effectively.

Department Two: The Department Of Optimism.

One of the secrets of the top 500 companies in the world is that each one of them is optimistic. They each see a wonderful future, no matter what is happening. They are optimistic when others are not. They know that after a big rain there will be a rainbow. If you are not very optimistic, you're going to eventually fail. You must be optimistic about yourself, your talent and your business, so others can be too.

Department Three: The Department Of Finance.

You have to have a very good relationship with money. You have to believe money is coming in, even when you might not exactly know where it's coming from.

You have to feel you will find the funds, because it's not cheap to become an actor. You need money for different type of acting classes, dance lessons, speech, private coaching, pictures, joining a fitness club, business clothes, transportation, and basic living expenses. You will have to invest money in yourself to make money. That's the only way you increase the value of your company.

Department Four: The Department Of Passion.

Your dream must be something you want to do more than anything in the world. It must be your life's mission or you will not succeed. If the dream is just a passing thought or idea, it will never become a reality. Passion pushes through any kind of negativity and any kind of "No!" you will hear along the way. (See the chapter "How To Turn A No! Into A Now!")

"If you are passionate about your life, then nothing will stop you from achieving your dream."

Department Five: The Department Of Training.

Every major company has training programs to teach their employees the latest techniques. I go around the world and teach employees how to better deal with their customers' needs. To maintain the edge in business you have to constantly be learning. If you're not training, you're not improving. You don't get better as an artist without training and practice. Al Pacino has had the same acting coach for the past 35 years. "I'm always open to learn," he told my actors. In Europe, where I have worked for years, actors don't realize that they need to continue their training. They get their diplomas and somehow think, "That's it, that's all I need". Imagine that you're going to have a doctor operate on you, but the last time he went to medical school was twenty years ago. Wouldn't you prefer to go to a doctor who learns the latest medical techniques each year? I know I would.

Department Six: The Department Of Risks.

The more risks you take, the more successful you will become. By taking risks you will live an exciting life. As an artist you have to feel that you're the exception to all the rules and that you are willing to do things that no one else is willing to do.

"The bigger the risk, the greater the reward."

Department Seven: The Department Of Happiness.

This is a very important department, which is most often neglected. If you don't have fun then you're going to burn out very fast. Bill Gates has a great long-term employee retention rate, because he treats his employees very well. He has gyms at the company and people can take time off for their families, if they need to. He realizes that happy people make better employees. Many people at other companies dislike their jobs, because they don't have a department of fun.

If you constantly work without taking care of yourself, you're not going to be productive. Stress is a killer. People who have fun are much more successful. Happy people will attract success. Some people think, "When I am successful, then I will be happy". That does not work.

(ᴖ☺☻ᴖ)

Happiness is not a destination, happiness is the way."

Department Eight: The Department Of Loving Yourself.

The more you love yourself the more we can love you. This is a message that you do not hear enough. You must learn to love and appreciate all the gifts that are inside you. Work on yourself everyday, because you are good enough and are only getting better. Change your attitude about yourself and it will change how others see you and ultimately change your future.

Department Nine: The Department Of Communication.

This could also be called The Department Of Relationships. How well do you communicate with other people? What kind of relationships do you currently have in your life? Are you a loner? Life and acting is about communication and if you are not constantly improving your communication skills, then you aren't becoming a better human being or a better actor. You should be able to convey your feelings, needs and wants effectively. This could be one of the most important departments you have, because how you communicate determines the quality of your life.

Department Ten: The Department Of Instincts.

The Department of Instincts works this way: You have a feeling to do something and you act on it. The opposite of that is logic, which rationalizes whether or not it is a good idea. Now, the brain will always see the negative side of things because its job, it feels, is to protect you from pain. Only by working on yourself can you ever get in touch with your instinct. The man who invented personal computers went to Hewlett - Packard and said, "I created a personal computer", and they said, "Who is going to want to buy that?" But, he had an instinct and decided to do it himself. Learn to listen and follow your instincts, they are always right.

CONCLUSION

Launching a successful acting career takes just as much effort as creating a successful business. You have to look at yourself as a product and create a business plan like corporations do. Are you trying to open up a little shop that may only have 15 minutes of success? Or do you want to launch an iconic business, which will be remembered throughout history?

Find Your Mission Statement.

Companies have corporate mission statements (what their goals are), and you need to have a personal mission statement too. To find your mission statement ask yourself the questions: "Why was I born?" "What am I here on earth to accomplish?" Your mission statement has to be so strong and powerful that you would be willing to die for it. It's like a quest. Something you don't need to be motivated to do. You work on it all the time. Write yours now! (For more information see "What's In It For The World" chapter).

THE BAD NEWS ABOUT TALENT!

When it comes to talent I have good news and I have bad news. The good news is you have talent. The bad news? So does everyone else! Every person is born with some kind of talent. Having talent in and of itself is not special.

What is special is the person who has the courage to see where their talent can take them. It is a shame that there are so many talented people, who are doing nothing with it.

My former acting teacher Milton Katselas once said, "You can access your talent only through having a *positive* attitude". The better the attitude the more talent you can access. Many actors think that they don't need daily practice. People also thought the earth was flat, they were wrong. Singers, dancers and musicians know that they must train everyday to stay great. To be a professional artist means making a serious commitment to your talent. The most successful people I know are successful not just because of their talent, but because they worked harder than anyone else. So, make sure you take that raw talent for a workout every day. That's the only way it's going to get stronger.

Here are some exercises that you must do regularly to develop and keep your talent growing. If you don't do them others will get the jobs you could have had. These tasks will help you become a better actor.

1. Take dance classes (like jazz) at least three times a week. Get in touch with your body. That is where your talent lives.

2. Take singing lessons. It doesn't matter how you sound, just sing and you'll find your inner voice.

3. Create an artistic family and read a play or script every week.

4. Read books about acting, success, life, anything. Always keep learning.

5. Enhance your five senses. Tell yourself that you don't hear, see, taste, smell or touch well enough. You must become more sensitive today than you were yesterday to become a better artist.

6. Check in on your emotions. Learn to deal with whatever is going on, don't avoid it. Pain and Anger will kill your career!

7. Go out and have some fun. Laugh a lot. Happy, creative people achieve their goals.

8. Go out into nature and see life from a different perspective. Find some quiet time to nurture your soul.

9. Go to a place where you can observe many people. Evaluate them as though you are going to write a book about them. Pay attention to their body, clothes, hairstyles, etc. See what is obvious and also note the subtext of their behavior. A person's body language can tell you 85 percent of who they are.

10. Work on scenes and do exercises that stretch you as an artist.

11. Dress up and play someone else for a day. Use a different voice or accent. Convince the world this is who you really are.

12. Talk to 3 people you don't know everyday. Open yourself up to a variety of personalities. Spend enough time with them, so that you can see yourself in them.

13. Travel to different places and explore the world. The more you know and experience, the more interesting you will become as a person and as an artist.

14. Play a bigger role in the world. Give your love, energy and talent to a charity or a cause. Remember, the more you give the more you will get.

15. Take different classes that inspire and scare you. That's the only way you will ever grow.

"You are either getting better or bitter. You don't ever just stay the same."

FAKING YOUR WAY THROUGH LIFE

"Acting - being someone other than yourself."

Most people go through life "acting" as someone other than who they really are. But only by taking the time to discover and embrace your truly authentic self, can you ever really succeed in your career and life.

Now, how will you know if you're faking your way through life? If you're not happy, not feeling powerful and not trusting your instincts, you're being someone else. It is easy to be lost, because most people have forgotten who their authentic self really is.

FINDING YOUR AUTHENTIC SELF

One of the problems I have as an acting teacher and success coach is dealing with people who think they are being authentic when they're not. I've discovered that most people don't know who they really are, so when I ask them to be authentic on stage or in business they have no idea what that really means.

Leonardo DiCaprio once told me that he only really started to work as an actor the moment he was willing to show the casting directors and producers his *authentic* self. He decided not to worry what anyone else thought about him. Leo is one of the most respected actors working in Hollywood today and he always puts his authentic self into his work.

Soon after we were born many of us were bombarded with negative messages about who we are, the way be behave, the way we react and the way we express our thoughts and feelings. Some were asked "What's wrong with you?" We're told, "Don't be like this" or "Don't be so emotional". This form of criticism comes to us from our parents or caretakers, and then from our friends and teachers. So, we started to think that what we were doing and feeling must be wrong. We've been taught to be ashamed of our bodies, thoughts, needs, ideas, instincts and finally ourselves. We started to disconnect from who we really were and began to develop a fake self that seemed to be more acceptable to the opinions of others. Most people lose their authentic selves soon after the age of 4 or 5, because they were told they had to behave a certain way to be accepted or loved. From then on they have spent a lifetime living this fake-self, because it gets a better response from other people they are in contact with. But, by behaving in this fake-self way, they receive things in their life that won't make them happy.

By continually empowering our fake-selves, we lose our inner strength and disconnect from the true purpose of our lives. We become disconnected from people and life. We become controlling and start to live in our heads. When we live in our heads we become negative, limited in our hopes and dreams, mediocre and finally become delusional about ourselves. We feel isolated from others. No longer in touch with reality, we become a divided person and are totally conflicted with our true self. It's a struggle inside that we keep losing. We become trapped in a collective coma where everyone is pretending to be someone other than themselves in order to fit in. Most people cannot ever escape the confines of their culture, family, friends or society. To be an authentic artist is to escape from this "collective coma" and join a minority group of authentic individuals that have the courage to be who they really are.

In order for you to reconnect, you will have to go deep within yourself to confront, acknowledge and change the things that you have been unwilling to face before. Many of these things you may not even be consciously aware of and you will need a coach to help you with this because alone you are unable to see all of your own blocks. The right mentor will help you to take steps towards productive change. This is serious work that must be done. But you will only discover who you are by going past your limited view of who you think you are.

"It is better to be disliked for what you are, than loved for who you are not."

—**Andre Gide**
French Novelist

43

To start the process of finding out your true self, there are some questions that you need to ask yourself. What are you most afraid of doing or showing on stage? I am talking about an action like maybe singing, dancing sexy, doing a stand-up routine, acting like a clown or playing a physically and mentally challenged character. You will have to perform the actions that scare you over and over again until you push yourself past your own boundaries.

Only by overcoming your blocks and fears will you discover your strength. (See the "Blocks And Fears Are Great" chapter.)

Many people become actors in order to become a different person; to get away from who they truly are. They do this because they don't like themselves, but acting is a journey *towards* yourself. You have to know and embrace who you really are, because you cannot bring truth to your acting if you don't know "the truth" about you. You could play a character by "pretending" to be that person, but that won't get you the job. People want you to reveal the part of yourself that is the character. You must allow yourself to feel all those emotions and explore all aspects of you. A composer cannot use a few notes to create a musical masterpiece and an actor cannot facilitate a great performance by only accessing a few parts of themselves. You will also find that the things you've been told are bad or wrong about you may actually be what makes you special. Once you are willing to embrace those special qualities, you will leave behind your fake-self and be on your way to finding your authenticity. I teach a famous German actress who as a child was always criticized for the way she laughed. When she became famous, her laugh became so popular that they turned it into a ring-tone, which her fans now download on iTunes. All successful artists bring their authentic selves into their work every day. So find your true self and share it with the world. There is no other choice.

"I studied with Bernard in Rome at my very first Masterclass and it really changed my life. After Rome I went to his London class because I knew I needed more. Two weeks after being with Bernard I got my first audition for a film and got the role. It was a miracle. I felt like a lion.

Bernard Hiller taught me how to believe. If you believe strongly enough, then it's going to happen. I have more energy and feel more vulnerable than I have in my entire life, and it is beautiful.

There is no one like him. He's got this special little key that opens our heart and allows you to find yourself and get in touch with your authenticity. He is a friend, not just a teacher. Bernard is going to change your life."

—Pasquale Greco
Italian - Actor

WHAT BLOCKS YOUR AUTHENTICITY?

H ere is a list of the blocks that stop you from becoming your authentic self. Until you deal with these blocks, you will not become the person or artist that you were born to be.

Block 1: The People Pleaser

This is the ultimate killer of authenticity. Now, there is a difference between those who are people pleasers and those who just like to please people. There is nothing wrong with pleasing people by entertaining them and making them feel good. But if you are a people pleaser, you are a person who is doing something you don't *really want to do* in order to make someone else happy. Inevitably this will make you angry and frustrated. The reason you are doing this is because you want to be loved. We are all in search of love. Always. But, when you're a people pleaser you neglect your needs and make the other person's wants and desires more important. You are hoping the other person will love and validate you, but of course that won't happen. You just end up being resentful and in pain, rather than receiving the love you are so desperately looking for.

Loving yourself is the key to everything. How much you love yourself is reflected directly in what you're willing to do for yourself and what kind of life you are willing to accept. There is a very strong connection between your self worth and the actions you are willing to take for your personal and professional improvement. How much time, money and education are you willing to invest in yourself? The better you feel about yourself the more you are willing to invest and therefore increase your self-worth. When you have a high self-worth it will give you the confidence to pursue your goals and dreams. In society there is a lot of negativity surrounding the idea of loving yourself. It is considered by many to be egocentric, selfish and self-centered, but they are wrong. Even the Bible says, "Love your neighbor as yourself". But how can you love your neighbor when you don't love yourself? You can't. The lack of self-love and appreciation is an epidemic problem in this world.

Block 2: Living in the past and future.

If you are stuck in the difficulties and problems of your past or living in fear of the future you will be lost and disconnected from your authenticity. Only when you are living in the present can you change and experience love and joy. For example, you could be on a beautiful beach, but you are unhappy. Why? Because you are thinking of a moment in the past in which someone hurt or caused you pain. When you are in your head you can never be in the moment. Only, when you are in this moment, the present, will you be able to see the beauty right in front of you. Being in the *present* is exactly that – a gift!

48

Do you love your work? Only when you love what you are doing can you be in the now. Many dream of being on stage, but then hold themselves back from being in the moment, because they are afraid of being judged or criticized. A great actor must bring the audience into the present moment with them. You must keep their attention or else their minds will wander. But, in order to bring them into the now, you have to live in the now yourself.

Block 3: Controlling personalities.

If you have a controlling personality, you feel that other people need to change, but you don't. You want things done exactly the way you want it and you are not willing to surrender to the moment. If you are not flexible and willing to go with the flow, you will fail. Your controlling personality does not allow anyone or anything in and therefore you have totally blocked yourself from success and living a meaningful and happy life. When you consciously give up control, you will be more open to life's opportunities.

Block 4: Needing to be loved at any cost.

When you're willing to give up too much of yourself to be loved or too much of yourself to be accepted by others you aren't able to be authentic. Some people are so desperate for love that they give themselves up completely to others. You need to give part of your heart away to be loved, but when you give everything away you are left with nothing. I have an acting student who met a girl who said she would be with him if he gave up acting. He told me he was really thinking about it. I said, "What are you figuring out? You're an actor! There is nothing to figure out! If you don't act, you are going to be unhappy for the rest of your life!" Who is going to want to live with a person like that?

Some people just push you to see how far they can go. These are people who don't have any boundaries. The same thing happens when parents expect their children to have an "acceptable" profession, and the children feel they have no choice but to conform to make their parents happy. But you have to ask yourself what is important to you. Do you just give up your dreams? Do you find a safe profession and dislike yourself for the rest of your life, or do you become the artist and person you are meant to be? Those are the choices you will have to make. If you make the wrong choice you will have to suffer the consequences forever. Remember whenever you become authentic and follow your heart, you will make some people very nervous and they won't be happy with you

Block 5: Too interested in what other people think and believe.

There are certain societies and cultures where one is told to always seek the advice and approval of others before taking any action. Then you start to feel that everyone seems to know more than you. You have to believe in your own instincts and choices. There are certain moments in life where no one can tell you what to do. You need to trust yourself. You will need to ask your own heart for advice. You can, however, look for words of wisdom only from those who have achieved what you desire. Why ask people who are living their nightmare to help you achieve your dream?

Block 6: Resistance to Change.

You are afraid to change, because you live in fear. You trust the past more than you trust your future. You think that by changing, you will lose all you have built for yourself. You want change as long as you don't have to change anything. Crazy, huh? You actually resist change, because you don't think you could deal with all the consequences that change will bring into your life. Change is too uncertain, too scary. You feel that it's better to stay the same than take full responsibility for your life. But life is change. If you don't allow yourself to change and grow you are going to miss your destiny. You will have to change to become your authentic self. There is no other way. Resistance to change always causes failure.

Block 7: Not having the courage to fully live your life.

Courage comes from the Latin word Coeur, meaning heart. So you must be very connected to your heart to live the life you were born to live. Pursuing your dreams is going to make you feel vulnerable. It takes courage to be vulnerable and believe in your dreams. It takes courage to be happy; to love or have faith no matter what is happening in your life. But remember no one is born with courage; courage is a choice. You could take a "safe" road and find a false sense of security. But, what you don't realize is that there are no safe roads in life and no place called "Security". Living a full and exciting life means taking lots of risks. Be brave and live the life that's right for your authentic self.

"Life is change. If you don't allow yourself to change and grow you are going to miss your destiny."

L.L.Cool J and Brett Ratner speak to the class

BLOCKS AND FEARS ARE GREAT

When it comes to blocks and fears people think, "Wow, those are terrible". But, the truth about all blocks and fears is that they are gifts from the soul. They have been placed in your way for you to start working on your personal growth. They are the things that you need to overcome to become powerful. Once you overcome your blocks and fears, you will discover your true inner power. And only powerful people can achieve anything. When people say to me, "I would like to have more confidence", I always reply, "You have to do things that you thought you were not capable of in order for you to expand and become the person you would like to be".

You should know that all fears are questions that need to be answered by you. When you say, "Can I make it in Show-Business?" You will need to find out if you can. Turn every fear into a question. If you don't answer that question, then all you are left with is the "Fear". You must answer the questions as they arise, because all your fears are just feelings, not facts. As a child you are born with only two fears: the fear of loud noise and the fear of falling. All other fears you now have, were given to you and accepted by you. Fears live in your head as thoughts that something in the future will not turn out well. The more you live in your head, the more fears you will have.

Blocks are limitations you have put upon yourself. A block such as, "I am not good enough", stops so many people, but of course you are good enough. Les Brown the motivational speaker says, "You have greatness inside." He is right, you need the courage to find it and then release that block.

So, blocks and fears are not negative. They're negative if you don't do anything about them, but they are liberating once you are on the other side of them. The way to live productively is to keep overcoming all the blocks and fears that will come to you for the rest of your life. That is when you grow and become the artist and the person you are meant to be.

> *"Here's to the crazy ones. The misfits. The rebels. The troublemakers. The round pegs in the square holes. The ones who see things differently. . . . You can quote them, disagree with them, glorify or vilify them. About the only thing you can't do is ignore them."*
>
> **—Steve Jobs**
> *Apple Computers.*

Dancing gets you into your body. That's where your talent lives.

UNLEASHING YOUR PINK ELEPHANT

O nce upon a time a pink elephant was born. He was so clearly different than the rest, that soon the grey elephants started to distance themselves from him and ignored him. The little pink elephant felt so sad and rejected. He realized that in order to fit in with the rest of the herd he had to be just like them. So, he covered himself with mud and dirt until he became grey. He went back to his friends and it seemed to him that they accepted him as one of their own. Throughout the years he kept covering himself and hiding behind the dirt. One day he saw a small herd of elephants in the distance. They were all pink. He realized that in fact he was just like them, but was too scared to show his real self. In that moment, rain began pouring down and washed away all the mud and dirt from his body. He was pink again. The grey elephants turned and started laughing at the sight of his pinkness. As the laughter grew louder, he realized that he was trying to fit into a group that would never understand him. There was no hiding any more. He knew that he was different and that he needed to find a group of pink elephants just like him where he would be accepted and learn to love himself.

Imagine yourself as an *"Elephant"*, the largest land animal on earth. An elephant is too massive to miss. It has an enormous amount of power. If you were a *"Pink Elephant"* when you were born, then you are different from most of the people around you. People will think that you are a bit strange when they meet you and because of this you may try to hide your true self. You try as hard as possible to fit in, but people always notice you. Sometimes you will be admired for being different, but often you will be ridiculed. In any case you will get a great deal of attention because you are so unique. Then, you have one of two choices to make. Either you gather strength and are proud that you are **Pink** or you try to convince everyone that you are exactly like them. Most choose the second option. It seems easier to just fit in.

If you are reading this, you probably are a "*Pink Elephant*" yourself. There comes a time when you have to strut your color. It doesn't matter that people will laugh at you, think that you are weird, or feel your dreams seem totally unattainable. You must not listen to them. They are too entrenched in the limited herd mentality to see the greater possibilities that are available. They will think that you don't have enough talent or know how to achieve your goals. Don't allow yourself to feel rejected by these limited members of society. Now, you must seek out places where you will find other Pink Elephants just like you, they are all around us. It will give you courage and strength to unleash the **"Pink"** elephant inside you.

I travel around the world and teach (hidden) Pink Elephants to become themselves. I bring them together and show them that they are not alone. They come alive in the presence of others just like them. Keep in mind that all the great inventors and innovators were Pink Elephants. It takes a unique person to get to the moon, be a music icon or create personal computers. The herd is always afraid of new ideas, but unabashed **"Pink Elephants"** are never stopped. Pink Elephants live in a world of possibilities, not fear.

Elephants are large and strong, but they can be contained. Baby elephants in circuses are tied to a steel pole soon after they are born, to keep them unaware of their power. When they are young, the small string tying them to the pole limits their movement. They buy into these restrictions and never realize their own strength as they grow. This scenario might describe you as well. You were taught limiting ideas as a child and you accepted these confines without question. But now, you will have to find the power inside you to break those ideas that hold you back to be able to achieve your heart's desires.

Pink elephants should never be ashamed of their unique ideas or view of the world. Pink is, after all, the universal color of love. So, unleash your Pink Elephant self and announce to the world "Here I am and this is me." Don't ever hold back your inner light. Let it shine out and give it to the world. Only then will you start to become fully alive. I have created Pink Elephant groups all over the world. Start one in your community today.

"What is different about you is what makes you special"

Pink Elephants celebrating their uniqueness in Tuscany!

ACTING IS A LIVING PROBLEM

The first part we play is the part we play in life. There is not a single day that goes by that we are not using acting to play different roles in our lives. We go from playing a father to a husband, from a mother to a wife, from a student to a teacher, and so forth. All we're doing is playing different parts of ourselves. Playing each character has different requirements and we switch effortlessly from one part to another throughout the day. *How well we play each part will determine our success in our life.*

> *"All the world's a stage and all the men and women merely players."*
>
> —Shakespeare

The moment a baby is born someone is given the part of a father or a mother. These new parents don't really know how to play these roles if they have never done it before. How well they learn to play their parts will determine the quality of life of the children they raise. Some children become very disappointed with their parents, because according to them, their parents didn't play the part as perfectly as they think they should have. This may be the way you feel about your parents, but did you play your part as perfectly as your parents think you should have played it? Now, I'm not saying that either one is right or wrong, but you each have your own expectations. When those expectations are not met, it leads you to express feelings of sadness, anger and frustration. If these issues and feelings are not dealt with, they will be brought into your life and block you from powerfully playing the parts in your own life. You are also connecting to the weakest part of yourself, which is why so many people don't succeed in this business. To pursue acting successfully, you must first connect to the strongest most powerful part of yourself. The most powerful electrical machine in the world that cannot find an outlet to connect to is worthless. Powerful people make powerful actors and weak people make weak actors. Which one are you?

"The most powerful electrical machine in the world is worthless, if it cannot find an outlet to connect to."

In the acting world, there is a common belief that having personal problems or traumatic experiences in life is not bad, because they could be brought into your acting work. That's true, but are you on top of your personal problems, or are your personal problems on top of you? If they are on top of you, you can't use them **because right now** they are using you. Only when you successfully work though your issues can you use your past personal problems for your work.

To be extraordinary in any role you want to play, you must train and find that part inside yourself. Only by working on yourself are you going to become a "professional" human being. Sadly, most people remain amateur human beings throughout their lives. What can you expect from an amateur? Not much. Professional humans are capable of achieving so much more

DON'T FORGET YOUR HUMAN NEEDS!

"Until you take care of your lower needs, you will never be able to fulfill your higher needs."

—Abraham Maslow

The reason most people never fulfill their dreams, goals or hopes is because their basic human needs are never met. Fulfilling these human needs will help you in dealing with your current problems or desires.

These ten needs listed below supersede any dream or goal that you might have. They are not optional; your body is constantly trying to fulfill them consciously or subconsciously.

THE TEN HUMAN NEEDS

Human Need One: Food And Water.

Your body is always in survival mode, constantly monitoring and thinking about food and water; where and when to get it. If you didn't know when you'll have your next drink or meal, then that would become your primary goal. You would spend all your time in search of these things and you would not be able to focus time on anything else.

Human Need Two: Clothing And Shelter.

What if you didn't know where you were sleeping tonight? Could you really concentrate on reading this book? One of the reasons that you feel calm enough to read this book is that you know where you are spending the night and you have clothes. Without clothes you couldn't even leave your house. Making money also becomes your focus in order to acquire these basic things.

Human Need Three: Sleep.

You can't live without sleep. Some people may think that sleep is a waste of time. But your body needs it. If you don't get enough rest your system won't regenerate and won't function at an optimum level. Eventually your body and brain will just shut down without sleep and you could even die.

Human Need Four: To Love And Be Loved.

We all need love; it is not a choice. You love because you have to, not just because you want to. Your body and mind are constantly trying to connect to others through love. You must be able to both give and receive love to be fulfilled.

Human Need Five: To Be Held And Touched.

This is a need that starts from the day you are born. The first thing a doctor does when a baby is born is put it in the mother's arms because it needs to be held. If you had a baby and gave it food, attention and clothing, but never touched it in the first year of its life, it could develop severe mental and physical problems. In some cases the baby could die. Touch is the only sense a child cannot live without, because being held and touched is crucial to survival. Studies have shown that the more children are held, the smarter and the more secure and confident they will be. Science suggests that you need at least five hugs a day. Are you getting yours?

Human Need Six: Acknowledging Your Pain.

Pain is a messenger that demands your attention. If you feel sad, angry, empty or lost, you are not acknowledging your pain. You are trying to do what most people do and just pretend that it doesn't exist. As much as you are trying to forget the pain, pain doesn't seem to ever want to forget you. Your body stores all the pain and traumatic experiences you have had in your entire life. Without acknowledging and releasing those feelings you cannot move on. You will be stuck in this need until you resolve it. Are you dealing with your pain?

Human Need Seven: Being Needed.

That is really what a family or community is about. A family structure is having the feeling that you are wanted and needed, and that you are stronger together than you are individually. If you don't feel that anyone needs you or anyone wants you, then there isn't really a reason to get up in the morning. There is nothing you can accomplish alone but in the right group you can achieve anything. You want to belong to a group that says, "We are so glad you're here", and when you find that group that makes you feel like that, you have found your creative family.

John Lennon once said:
*"A dream you dream alone is only a dream,
but a dream you dream together becomes reality."*

Human Need Eight: Creating A Life Of Meaning.

There is a wonderful book entitled "Man's Search For Meaning" by Viktor Frankl. It describes a man who is trying to survive his brutal experience in a World War II concentration camp, because he wanted his life to have meaning. When you have meaning and purpose in your life, you get up in the morning with an energy that is unstoppable. If you don't know your purpose, then you are just aimlessly wandering around without any direction. You are constantly asking, "Why am I here?" We all want to know that our lives have meaning. The more meaningful your life is, the happier you will become.

Human Need Nine: Optimism.

We are all born wanting to be happy. An optimist sees possibilities and finds hope in the most difficult of times. You can't live without hope; it is what keeps you going. Hope makes you believe that everything is possible. We are naturally attracted to positive, hopeful and optimistic people because that is our true nature. Having a dream is not special, what is special, is the person who sees the beauty and possibilities in their dreams.

Human Need Ten: Love And Trust Yourself.

When you love and trust yourself, you connect to your instincts and follow the messages of your heart. Remember, your heart will not lead you astray and your instincts will help you fulfill your bliss. You must learn to love yourself and appreciate everything you have to offer. You are working on yourself through love. By loving and trusting yourself you connect with a higher part of yourself. When you learn to trust yourself, you will know how to live.

The Dream:

Realize that these ten human needs are constantly working to fulfill themselves. Only when you satisfy these needs can you focus your energy and power towards your dream.

> *"To work with Bernie is an emotional journey of depth, laughs, fear, jumping in the emptiness and trusting in your possibilities. Not in a blind childish way, but in a committed, responsible and artistic way. I am happy to have him as a friend and a true professional."*
>
> —**Joaquin Perles**
> Spanish Actor

Producer Barry Navidi, "The Merchant of Venice" speaks of the need for "Passion, Persistence, Perseverance and above all Patience"

THE ACTING LOVER

Acting is like a relationship with a lover, it demands your constant attention. Ask yourself the question: What are you willing to do for your lover to show him/ her that you are very serious about this relationship? Know that everyday your acting lover will be testing your commitment. Once a month is not enough to show your lover how serious you are about this relationship. You must create evidence everyday to convince your lover that you are sincere. If the relationship fails, it's because you did not show enough commitment and love.

Below are 15 things you must do to show that you are committed to this "lover".

1. You're up by 6 am to start your day.

2. You're positive and you expect miracles.

3. Never late to any appointments.

4. You work out - You stay in shape!

5. You do something every day to help your career. Be it lessons or group classes.

6. You have a readiness, a trust, and flexibility to whatever comes your way.

7. Don't tell everyone you want to be an actor. You just do it!

8. Learn how to be a better communicator, so you can get the things you need.

9. You seek solutions for your problems. You talk *to* your problems, not *about* them.

10. You don't wait; you start to live your dream today!

11. You keep creating your own opportunities.

12. You surround yourself with beauty and motivated artists.

13. You bring lots of passion to everything you do.

14. You become the person that people want to meet and work with.

15. You burn your lifeboat so you have no choice but to achieve this. You have no back-up plan.

With Actor-Director Nikita Michalkov in Moscow.

"The camera can film my face
but until it captures my soul,
you don't have a movie."

Legendary Al Pacino

WORDS ARE NOT THE TRUTH

As an artist understanding the truth is your most powerful weapon.

One of the reasons people go to see films, television or theatre is they are looking for *truth*. The truth is something that is so rare in life that if you see or hear it, you can't look away. Audiences come to learn more about themselves and to connect to the story in a way, which relates to them. Through the actors they are given permission to feel a rainbow of emotions. These powerful art forms bring the world together and help us see ourselves and life's possibilities in a new light.

The most common mistake many actors make when getting a script is, they assume that what they are saying is the "truth", but words are never the whole truth. What I'm speaking about is something that is **beyond** sub-text. Your job as an actor is to find what the character really is wanting, meaning, feeling and going through because in life we often don't speak the truth. Additionally, sometimes what you are saying in the scene is totally not true at all. Under pressure, people have trouble expressing how they feel in words. I would say that the script is only thirty five percent of the truth. You will need to find the remaining sixty five percent yourself. You can only do this by knowing a lot about life and therefore understanding human interactions.

Words can be the worst way to communicate, because words alone are symbols that have no meaning until you give them significance. So it depends what you are hearing and what you think they may mean. Let's take a word like *love*. That's a powerful word and if you look up love in the dictionary there are so many different definitions. You can tell someone, "I love you", but they will have to choose, which love you meant. Are you talking about friendship? Did you really mean "lust"? Did you use the wrong word? Did you mean "like" and used "love" instead? These are questions you will have to ask yourself. Maybe you aren't in love at all, but are using that word to manipulate their behavior. Trying to figure this all out in a scene will add to the richness of your work. (A great acting teacher can help with this.) Life can be very complicated, because most people are not articulate enough to use the right words in expressing their feelings and some people are not in touch with what they are feeling.

You may have a couple arguing in a scene, for example, telling each other how they are not right for one another. So, you may think that the scene is about a breakup. But in truth it's about two people desperately trying to stay together. If they really knew they were not right for each other, there would be nothing to argue about and they would just leave. You only argue with people you care about and about things you care about. To be a great actor is to understand the truth better than anyone.

So here is a secret, in every scene you're always fighting for something that is missing – and that something is - **LOVE**. Where is the love in the scene? Everyone in life wants to be loved. Even scenes that appear to have no love are actually all about love. If you loved me, you would understand what I want and why I want it. If there is anger in a scene remember that behind anger there is hurt and behind that hurt there is a need to be loved. Love is the root of all action. Once you can understand the role love is playing in your own life, you can understand more about the truth. *To be a great actor is to understand the truth better than anyone else.*

Start reading a lot of books and watching shows on human psychology and sociology. You need to be aware why people do the things they do. Also know that if we told people the total truth all the time, about how we feel about them, we would lose a lot of friends. In life we have to figure out how to express ourselves and still maintain our relationships.

There are some people who are completely unconscious of the fact that what they think about life and themselves is nowhere near the truth. I see it every day. I do an exercise in my classes where students express their feelings. Some say how happy they are, but I can see that they are completely disconnected, sad and lying to themselves. Many people say to me, "I want to be a great actor". But I can tell you that seventy five percent of the people who come to me and say, "I am really serious about acting", are not. They're just wanting to be famous and adored, not become actors. They don't understand the amount of work and commitment that becoming a great actor takes.

"The truth is something that is so rare in life that if you see or hear it, you can't look away."

—Howard Fine

The Fifth Level Of Truth

One of the things that I talk about is what I call, the fifth level of truth. Once you arrive at the fifth level of truth you have found the **Real Truth**. You have to be a detective and investigate further into the motivations behind the actions of a scene by finding the "Why". When you ask yourself, for instance, "Why do I like making love?" Many answers will come your way, but the fifth answer, the deepest answer, will be the most truthful. The truthful answer also happens to be an answer to which every person on the planet would say "yes" to.

To get to that truth you must ask yourself "Why" at least 5 times. Most people will say they like to make love because it feels good. Then I ask, why does it feel good? "It feels good because it makes me feel free." Ok, why do you like to feel free? "Because I feel open and connected to another person." "Why do you like to feel open and connected to someone?" "Because it makes me feel loved." "Why do you like to feel loved?" Now we come to the fifth answer and this is the answer to why everyone in the world likes to make love. "Because it makes me feel alive." That is the ultimate truth. Most people only acknowledge the first two levels, but artists must find the true meaning behind their behavior. This investigation will give you a great insight into your characters' needs and actions. So, now you understand why people are really doing what they are doing. The first four answers to your "why?" are about twenty percent of the truth, but the fifth answer is always the real truth. The deeper you go, the more powerful an artist you can be, because it's not just *your* truth, but also everyone's truth.

Say you are playing a detective trying to interrogate a murder suspect. What does the detective want? The first level of truth is to solve the case. This will make for a one noted performance. So let's investigate. The better choice will be to find a deeper truth, therefore increasing the stakes.

For example, if he doesn't get the suspect to confess, he will be fired and won't be able to support his wife and kid. Then he will feel like a failure and less of a human being. He feels scared for the first time in his life, by the one criminal that he can't seem to understand. And finally he wants to solve his case because he wants his life to have meaning and purpose. These are all deeper truths than what's on the page. Remember, the more you discover the greater and richer the performance.

You may play a character, who is dating a different person every night and you may think that this person must be very happy and free. But, when you look at the fifth level of truth you realize that he or she is doing this, because they feel so dead and worthless inside that they must connect with someone to feel alive or important. The fifth level of truth will bring a character's motivations to the forefront in a profound way. For you to give an unforgettable performance you will need to find and play the fifth level of truth. Here are some truths that will help bring out a dynamic portrayal.

1. Emotional Truth

We are primal, instinctual and emotional beings. If we allow ourselves to feel the true feelings we have about a particular thought or event, we will connect to the truth. If we intellectualize it we will disconnect. But one of the things about feelings is that they change every moment. One minute you like something and the next minute you don't. Feelings are like a river that constantly flows. The way you're feeling about anything or anyone always changes. It gets more intense or less intense. You're certain of some feeling or perception you have and then you're less certain of that feeling and perception you have. Find the emotional river inside you and you'll discover amazing moments. The moment you try to plan an emotion instead of just letting the feeling come to you, your acting will be seen as fake and superficial. In acting you don't focus on the feelings, but on why you desperately want something which forces you to action and if the stakes are high enough in the scene, emotions will come. (Also find strong personal meaning, which brings heat to the scene.)

2. Physical Truth

Ninety-two percent of human communication is non-verbal. Expressing yourself with words can be complicated, which is why physical or visual contact is so important. When people are not saying what they feel, we can see the truth by watching their body language. Your body never stops expressing itself. What's yours saying?

3. Ways Of Finding The Truth

The more you know the "Real Truth" about yourself, the more you will know it about someone else. You then can bring that insight and that knowledge to your work. The next chapter lists 25 questions that will get you more in touch with the truth about you.

Great acting is not simple. The great artists spend a lot of time trying to find out everything about the character they are playing, beyond just the details in the script. Whatever character you play has had a whole life before the events written on the page. You have to come to this moment as an actor knowing as much as you can about the character's past, so that you can deal with his/her present. If you don't understand your characters past you will be very confused. Actors with amnesia make for lousy acting. (See next chapter "Amnesia Make For Lousy Acting.") So, you need to understand everything about this character - how you think, what you like/dislike, what their life was up until this moment, where they are going, what they dream about and bring that knowledge to this event.

"As an artist, understanding the real truth is your most powerful weapon."

AMNESIA MAKES FOR
LOUSY ACTING

If you are like most people, you don't really know that much about your real self. So, how are you supposed to connect to an invented character you are playing? You must regularly go deep inside yourself to understand who you really are and why you are behaving in a certain way. When you are out of touch with yourself you will only be able to give superficial performances.

People are looking for the real thing. Some say that acting has gotten so bad that Reality TV is taking over the airwaves. Something is not right. Audiences would rather watch "real" people living in a house, than watch a scripted TV show. Reality TV is a reaction to audiences yearning for more truth.

Actors must bring back Reality *and* Truth into their work. (That's where the magic lies). If we don't, we will lose our viewers and our livelihood. There is nothing more wonderful then seeing an exhilarating performance. **"A great actor can teach you how to live."** Do not perform until you have answered all the following questions! They will help you connect to the "Fifth Level of Truth". (Read previous chapter)

[the questions as you can about yourself,
w about you, the more you will be able to find
you are playing.

uestions about the character you are playing
and make complicated non-logical choices. The more dynamic the
choice, the more dynamic the performance.

"Talent is in the choices you make."
—Stella Adler

1. What is your family name? Where were you born? How did
    the place and your last name affect you?

2. What did your mother and father do? How do you feel
    about them? Did they love you? Did you love them?

3. What did you have to do to be loved by your parents? How
    did you have to act or behave to be appreciated by others?

4. What kind of childhood did you have? What were the
    lessons you were taught?

5. What was the best and worst incident in your childhood?

6. How do you feel about your brother and sister? Or how do you feel about being an only child?

7. What makes you laugh, angry, afraid or cry? What turns you on?

8. What were the relationships that have defined your life?

9. When and with whom were you first in love? What does love mean to you?

10. Where and when was your first sexual experience? How was it? What does sex mean to you? How do you use it?

11. What is your body language telling the world? Where do you walk from? Head– Heart – Sex?

12. What is it about your body you like? What don't you like?

13. What do you think is your best quality? (Funny honest...)

14. What do you think is the least attractive part of your personality? (Impatience, negativity...)

15. What part of yourself do you try to hide from others? What are you ashamed of?

16. What are your fears and blocks, and how are they stopping you?

17. What is the contradiction in your personality?

18. What are you addicted to? Drugs, Money, Fame, Pain, Sex, Power, Work...?

19. What is your philosophy of life? Where did that come from? Family, Friends, Culture?

20. What were your first goals or dreams? Are you pursuing them? If not, why not?

21. List 3 life-changing events, positive and negative, that are still affecting you today?

22. How do you feel about change? Are you a master or a victim of change?

23. What is preventing you from being more authentic in your life?

24. Who do you admire in life and why?

25. How would you like to be remembered?

You must personally identify with the event and the character. Otherwise there won't be any vulnerability in your performance. The more personal and meaningful, the better! Only when you know your character inside out, will you be free to just **be**!

(ᴖ◕‿◕ᴖ)

"Great acting can teach people how to live."

"I first saw Bernard on a German TV-show called "Mission Hollywood". He sat on the Jury of 3 and he was the only one that told the truth about the actors that he saw. That was fantastic. I loved him from this moment on. I wrote an email and I asked if he wanted to come to Germany and give a class at my acting studio. And he did. My students and I were hooked from the first moment he started speaking. Now, I can't live without his training."

—**Bernd Capitain- German**
Actor and Teacher

Judge on Mission Hollywood with actor Til Schweiger

HOW TO GIVE AN UNFORGETTABLE PERFORMANCE

T he way to become successful in Show-Business is to be willing to be different. One place for an actor to demonstrate this uniqueness is at auditions and performances. Every actor has to present themselves in front of producers, directors, executives, and casting directors to get a job. To become unforgettable you have to ask yourself, "How would everyone else play this role?" This is what I call the "Universal Choice"; the way everyone else would play this part. Once you figure that out, you need to make a totally different choice. (You may need an acting coach to help you with this). But this will get you noticed.

For example: If a script says you need to be angry at a certain moment then the unique choice might be, not to do that. Everyone who comes in the room will play it that way, but if you display the opposite emotion – calm - and can make that choice work in the scene, it will make you unforgettable. Your job as an actor is to enhance the script and bring something to it that no one else even thought was there. Certainly if you're going in to play a few lines, you will have to do it as written. But, if you surprise them with something a bit different they might take notice. They may want you to eventually play the "Universal Choice", but they will be impressed with a well-executed creative choice.

"Every great idea starts as a dream."

Many great actors got their first big break when they played contrary to the expectations of the role. Sharon Stone once told me the story of her audition for her big breakthrough film called "Basic Instinct". Now when you think of the character she played, a seductress and murderer, would you think this is a comedy or a drama? Most people would say, well it's a drama. But she didn't think it was a drama. If you go on *You Tube* and see her screen test for this movie, you will see that she and her acting coach the late Roy London thought it was a comedy. Throughout this entire audition, they are accusing her of murder and she just smiles, laughs and plays it light. That is what made her audition so special. She told me that she heard lots of actors in the audition room play it like an intense drama. They didn't get it.

When you think of unforgettable roles, such as, Hannibal Lecter in Silence of the Lambs, how would most people play it? Others would play him like an animal, scary and intimidating. But what did Anthony Hopkins do? He played it sophisticated, charming and very calm.

He was completely still, and that opposite choice was frightening.

When an audience sees a character, they have expectations on how that character will behave, but once you play it differently than what they expect, you get the audience's attention. Reacting to events in the script in a different way impresses the audience as well. Watch Marlon Brando in "On The Waterfront" and you'll see what I mean. He is always reacting to the other actors in surprising ways.

The better choices you make, the more talented you will appear. You will need an acting teacher who can give you some choice ideas on how to play a part, because one "great idea" can win you an Academy Award.

If you want to be unforgettable you have to risk not being popular. Jack Black told me that when he used to go to auditions, people thought he was too big. Everyone including his agent said, "Why don't you just calm down when you audition", but he kept embracing his authentic self and that is what made him successful; his willingness to take a chance on himself. It takes courage to take a character and risk failure in order to bring something to the script that no one has ever seen, it takes courage to be unforgettable. Believe in yourself and go against the grain. Here is a list of the most effective ways to create your unforgettable performance.

"The better the technique; the better the actor."

NEEDS FOR A SCENE

1. **Emotional Objective:** Something you want from the other person that would make you *Emotional* if you got it or if you didn't get it. There is something you want them to **Do** and something you want them to **Say**, the more difficult the better. You must also know before coming into the scene that the other characters in the scene feel and think opposite from you. You have to convince them to give you what you want; Now! You're in a Crisis.

    All scenes are emergency moments in your character's life played out calmly.

2. **The Moment Before:** Where are you coming from?
    The character has had a life up to this point. <u>You must come into the scene loaded</u> with physical, emotional and verbal needs that need to be fulfilled now.

3. **Obstacles:** Yours and Theirs. These are things that stand in the way of you getting what you want. The greater the obstacle to overcome, the greater the performance. You must have internal obstacles as well as external. Such as feeling lost and confused and never knowing what to say. The inner struggle is just as strong as the outer struggle. Where is the *conflict* in the scene?

4. **Tactics**: These are different ways in which you are trying to get what you want. What is your way of getting what you want in the scene? Using sex, intellect, humor, sadness, manipulation, anger or guilt? Observe a teenager trying to borrow the car from his parents and you will learn about tactics. The more interesting the tactics the more compelling you will be.

5. **The WHY:** You must know **WHY** you need what you want in this scene. Don't plan on **HOW** you are going to get it. If you play the **HOW**, it will be superficial. When you find the **WHY**, there is more excitement in watching you. You will also find your motivation in the scene. **WHY** are you saying or acting like this **NOW**? The **WHY** must engage your heart/gut, not your head.

6. **The Stakes**: When the stakes are very high, every moment means something. What can you lose? That's what motivates you to start the scene. You must be able to lose big so that you can win big. The higher the stakes the more interest the audience has in your scene. The loss must be very meaningful to you personally. High Stakes give excitement to any scene.

7. **Personalize:** The objective and the story. It must be something you can understand or be able to relate to. The more personal it is to you, the more meaningful it will be to others.

8. **Words are not the truth**: What you are saying is not exactly the truth. Find the true meaning of your lines. Such as "I never want to see you again?" could mean. "I cannot live without you". Getting to that fifth level of truth will reveal the dramatic moment. (See chapter "Words Are Not The Truth.")

Remember: What your partner is saying is, 25% true! We only argue and fight for something because it's meaningful to us.

"Play the scene the writer should have written but didn't.
Never play the plot. That plays itself."

9. **History**: Who are you? (The human being - not just the character.) What is the history of the other person in the scene? Did you answer the 25 Questions in the previous chapter? Then you can just "**Be**" that person, not "**Act**" that person. Audiences want the real thing, which can only happen when you are in a state of "Being".

10. **Arc**: Where is the ARC in the scene? You must start in one place emotionally and end in another. There are Physical arcs as well. Perhaps you start off tense and you become calm. But it must flow from one thing to another.

11. **The Event**: What is happening in this scene that has never happened before? Find the uniqueness of this moment.

12. **Inside – Outside Acting:** On the outside you show one thing on the inside you feel totally different; like a pressure cooker or a volcano. Calm on the outside and boiling on the inside. Cool on the outside and nervous on the inside. The inside wants to express itself, but doesn't. That is what people do everyday, they learn to hide their true feelings and emotions.

13. **Instincts:** React with your impulses! Shock yourself. Don't be logical. Nobody is.

14. **Point of View:** It's very important to promote your character 's point of view. You never judge your character. Every person in the world always thinks what they are doing is right. Whether they are good or bad, you must promote your view in the most positive way to get the changes you want from the other person. You must actually fall in love with your character 's needs and wishes.

"Always expect that the person is going to say and do the opposite thing to what you expected of them."

—**Uta Hagen**

15. **Activity.** What are you physically doing in the scene? Would you have kept doing it if that person did not come into your space? Activities can reveal to the audience how you really are feeling at the moment, because the body never lies.

16. **Acting is Reacting**. Everything you say is in reaction to what the other person is saying or doing. Take your partner's behavior and dialogue personally. (When you are just concerned about your own performance, you are disconnected from the scene). Find the Trigger words in the scene. Which words set you off? React to everything.

"Listen with your blood."
—**Stella Adler**

17. **Not knowing what to say:** You always have two thoughts that the character is thinking coming at you at the same time. You don't know which one to say, and at the last second, one of them comes out. When you are lost and unsure how to answer, that creates tension.

18. **Winning:** How are you trying to *win* in the scene? We love to watch winners. The better actor in the scene is the one that achieves his goals even under impossible situations.

Find the power in the silence. Some of the most impact-full moments in our lives are in silence. Don't speak unless you can improve on the silence.

"*Never play victim.*"

—**Ivana Chubbuck**

WHY ARE THE COMFORT ZONES SO UNCOMFORTABLE?

There comes a time in your life where you feel that you are in a "comfort zone". It is a place where you have stayed far too long. Your heart says there is more to life than this, but your brain says, "Don't rock the boat, play it safe, and keep what you have." You will have to move out of your comfort zones to achieve more in your life or your career.

In life you will constantly be entering comfort zones. If you refuse to leave, these comfort zones will become the "dead zones". No matter how good it might be where you are now you will ultimately be in the comfort zone and that will cause you pain and disappointment. You will know you are in a "dead zone" because you function without energy and lack of purpose in life. It's an awful place to be. Unfortunately, so many people in this world accept such a place as "normal".

We live in a world where fear is the dominant feeling, so to counterbalance that, you seek a "false" sense of security. You like to stay in places called comfort zones, because to go from the known to the unknown is too scary and too risky. You fear that you could never find a better job, relationship opportunities. You are too frightened to move or change your life, because you believe that whatever is coming next, will never be as good as what you have now. But that is not the truth. We were created with limitless possibilities. The way to achieve this is to break through your **own** fears so that you can accomplish your goals. And remember fears are just feelings not facts. It's only a matter of time before you realize that you must leave these comfort zones because you are getting more uncomfortable there every day. So, stop suffering and start to move now!

You must become optimistic and trust that things will work out. Only then will you be vulnerable enough to move into the **unknown**. It is only in the unknown where everything is possible and exciting. It is the only place where you can start to build and fulfill your dreams. Remember you are either building your dreams or your nightmares. What are you building?

"In order to discover new lands, one must be willing to lose sight of the shore."

—Andre Gide - French Writer

Simon Beaufoy won an Oscar for writing "Slumdog Millionaire" and spent invaluable time in several of my London classes.

DON'T TALK TO STRANGERS

To become successful in Show-Business you must talk to a lot of people that you don't know. Hollywood is a town that runs on connections. You will need to find and create a team that believes in you. I have met so many students who think they can achieve success by being alone. The only thing you can ever accomplish alone in life is sadness and failure. You will need lots of help from others to achieve something great.

Now, how you first approach someone will determine your success or failure in your endeavor. Everyone judges you by your first impression and you never get a second chance to make a first impression. So, as you walk up to somebody, ask yourself this question: "Is this person I'm going to talk to someone I know, like a friend or are they a stranger? If you decide that they are strangers you will act "strange" when you speak to them. If you decide that they are friends you will act "friendly" toward them. Remember, they will have the same response toward you. Which do you think will be more productive? Of course, friends. How do you enter a room full of good friends? Happy, open and excited to speak to them.

Now, some of you may say, "But I don't know this person that I'm going up to talk to". Is that really true? You don't know them? What is it that you don't know about them? All human beings all over the world have the same needs and desires. Everybody wants to be loved, accepted and understood. **EVERYBODY.**

Successful people see themselves in everyone they meet. Unsuccessful people always feel that they are totally different and that nobody will understand them. By really looking and connecting with people you will be able to understand 85% of who they are and what they are feeling. Find people interesting and they will find you interesting.

One of my teachers once taught me that you should know at least 2 minutes on every topic in the world, so that when you meet people you can talk about anything. So, get busy learning lots of new things. How you communicate in life will determine the degree of success you will have. So, start speaking to people that you don't know. That is the only way you will keep improving the art of communication. Remember your mother was right; never talk to strangers, only talk to people you know.

"Prior to meeting Bernie I wasn't sure what I should do or how I was going to live my life. There were things I wished for and dreamed of doing, but never had faith in myself to do them. I was mostly negative. I listened to all the things that anyone has ever said to me. As much as I always wanted to be my fun wacky self and be performing, I didn't have the courage to do so. Bernie really helped me to believe in myself and see the talent that I have within. He brought everything out. "No more hiding, no more masks. Take it all out and be truthful with yourself. Be vulnerable and let people in."

I have now been living in "uncertainty" and it's been so amazing. I see the possibilities. I have always wanted to be so creative in every single aspect of my life and after working with Bernie I have accepted that I am a writer, a director, an actress and a painter. I learned that I could be everything. I now write screenplays to express myself and to potentially change the lives of others. I thank God that I met him."

—**Emma Jacobs**
Hollywood Actress

"Bernie takes dreams and converts them to actions".
Paul Haggis - Academy Award Director/Writer
"Crash", "Million Dollar Baby"

OPPORTUNITIES NEVER KNOCK

Opportunities don't knock, they whisper. To be in touch with your opportunities you will need a quiet mind and a sensitive soul. Only by eliminating anger, hostility, negativity and sadness you will be able to connect with your opportunities, otherwise you will miss them.

"The most expensive thing in life is a missed opportunity."

INSTINCTS WILL LEAD YOU TO OPPORTUNITIES.

You can't see or touch instincts. They often generate seemingly illogical feelings. If you are living in your past or worrying about the future, you will never hear or feel your opportunities coming. Only when you are living in the now, are you able to be in touch with them.

Many people are stopped because they hide behind their logical mind, which always doubts you. But, you will need to connect to your instincts in order to achieve your dreams. Know that every great idea starts as a dream. J. K. Rowling first started writing her ideas on bar napkins. She believed so strongly in her book, even when several publishers turned her down because they felt it was too silly. Now they are the legendary Harry Potter series.

The most common blocks people have, is being stuck behind the blame game. "I don't have time." "I don't have enough money." "I can't do this because I don't know what to do." "I don't have any supportive people around me." None of these situations can stop someone who truly believes.

"Be the change you want to see in the world. Be the person you are looking for."

—**Gandhi**

You must get solutions to your personal problems to achieve your potential. Stop giving away your power and missing more opportunities. Know that if you don't take the opportunity that was meant for you, someone else will. If you miss your opportunities, you will miss what life has in store for you.

Opportunities are everywhere. They come in all kinds of shapes and sizes. Be ready to receive them. They will sometimes come from places you don't expect. Remember, every great idea comes with an equal amount of negativity, trying to stop you. The negativity is there to challenge you and see how much you really want something.

Think about an opportunity that you missed in your life, and think about why you didn't take it. Can you imagine what your life would have been like if you had taken it? Every opportunity is forcing you to learn and expand.

Five Lessons Opportunities Are Forcing You To Learn!

You will have to learn these lessons below to live the life you always wanted. "You will not be able to achieve your dreams by remaining who you are". You will have to grow!

Lesson One. Opportunities are forcing you to be more courageous. In the beginning you will only need to find 20 seconds of courage to see where your opportunities can take you. Remember no one is born with courage – courage is a choice.

Lesson Two. Opportunities force you to change and start living in uncertainty. You will have to change the way you think or the way you live or the way you respond, or all of the above. If you refuse to change you will fail in life, because a successful life is all about change.

Lesson Three. Opportunities force you to connect to your instinct. Trust your instinct; it's trying to help and guide you. Your mind lives in fear, it is not your friend, it resists because it's only interested in a "perceived" safety, which doesn't exist. Instinct lives in your heart and will show you the path to your dreams.

Lesson Four. Opportunities force you to believe in yourself more. You must increase your self worth to increase your life.

Lesson Five. Opportunities force you to take action and stop finding excuses for inaction. Start taking action now; always start before you are ready!

"When you trust in yourself, you trust in the wisdom that created you."

—Wayne Dyer

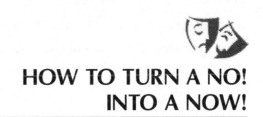

HOW TO TURN A NO!
INTO A NOW!

Neil Simon once said, "If anything can stop you, it's not for you." This is absolutely true.

If you're pursuing a dream and a "No!" can stop you, then the truth is, it's not for you. People who know WHY their dreams are important to them are unstoppable. One of the things you will hear throughout your entire life is the word "NO!". When average people hear that, they accept it, stop pursuing their dream and believe it is impossible. If you can't overcome that simple two-letter word, nothing will manifest itself in your life.

However, if you add the letter "W" to the word "No!" it becomes "NOW!"

I have taught my actors and students that when they hear "No!" they need to think that the person just said "NOW!" Their job is to push their agenda even further and find a way to connect with the person to change their mind. Saying "No!" has become an automatic response for so many people across the world. If you just keep on trying to turn a "No!" into a "NOW!" eventually people will say "Yes!", so never give up. Over the years we have been lucky to have some of the top industry professionals and Oscar winners attend my classes as guest speakers. Do you think they all said yes when I asked them to attend? No!

For practice I tell my students to go to the best restaurant in town, where it may take months to get a reservation, and go eat there tonight. Your job is to change the Hostess' answer from a "No, I'm sorry we are totally booked!" to "Yes, right this way!" You will only achieve this with *charm, humility* and *humor.* If you can't get a table at a busy restaurant, can you really have a successful acting career?

Find the fun in overcoming each obstacle and find new tactics to overcome them. You might disturb some people along the way, but as the old saying goes, "You can't make an omelet without cracking a few eggs". I guarantee you that you will feel a lifetime of regret for all the things you did not do.

"Life is making mistakes and death is wishing you made more."

Director - Andy Tennant

Every great actor has been told "No!" more times than they would ever like to remember, but what made them great in addition to their talent was their ability to turn a "No!" into a "NOW!"

**A group of actors who overcame "No!"
in the London Masterclass!**

"If you make the easy choices in life, you'll have a hard life.

But if you make the hard choices in life, you'll have an easy life."

—Les Brown

113

WHAT'S IN IT FOR THE WORLD?

In my acting classes I always ask the students to tell me how the world benefits if they became successful as an actor.

Truthfully, most people look a bit confused about this question. They generally respond, "Well, I just want to work that's all". But I always inform them that to be successful in Show-Business, the audience must benefit from what you are offering. If you are joyous, vulnerable, authentic and speaking the truth with love, they will respond to you. Every product (which you are) becomes successful when the people love it. What do you bring that's desirable?

What is your mission statement? To succeed, you will need to find a mission statement that benefits others. (To learn more about Mission Statements, see page 35).

Are you here to give hope and inspiration to people just like you? To show others that if you can make it, so can they? Are you willing to tell your personal story so that it would benefit others? Do you want to create a film or a play that brings focus to something in the world, which you feel is not getting enough attention?

I believe that artists should use their talents to change the world with their art. I know that some teachers don't think so. But I feel artists can make a big difference in this world. So... I ask you this important question:

"Why does the world need you to be an artist?"

For example:

"I want to create adventure films that allow people to live in their imaginations and escape into another world for a moment."

"I want to have people across the world embrace themselves for who they really are, and through comedy allow them to embrace the message of "Don't take your life so seriously. Have fun and enjoy the ride.""

These are profound statements that are much greater than the individual and will give you purpose, meaning and the passion to succeed. Why does the world need actors at all? This can be answered with the simple statement "Know Thyself". We are, in a sense, prisoners trapped in our own minds, perpetually alone with ourselves.

There is a desperate need in all human beings to ease this loneliness by creating bonds with other people, sharing experiences, thoughts and beliefs. To experience a deeper level of connection we have a need to share our thoughts about life with everyone in the world. One of the ways in which we do this is through the performing arts.

We have to realize that despite physical appearances, we are all fundamentally the same in our desires to be loved, understood and accepted. That is why art transcends all race, gender, language, religion and culture. Through art we share our fears, desires, needs, perversions, fantasies, greed and lust. When we watch a film, see a play or listen to a singer that resonates within us, we feel less alone. We feel as though someone understands us. Compassion and a deeper understanding of others can heal the world. This, in my opinion, is the greatest gift we can give each other.

If I can bring a character to life and that character can touch the heart of another, and somehow inspire them to feel less afraid and more connected to the world, then I must do this! To hold back and fail would be a tragedy. I am part of a living tradition, a legacy that must be guarded and maintained with absolute ferocity. I am so grateful that I've been given the gift to be an artist.

Celebrating a performance of "Homage to Acting"
in the center of Rome with my actors from all over the world.

THE BENEFITS OF NEGATIVITY

B ENEFIT - Something that is advantageous or positive for *you* in some way. Other people might not see the benefits of your behavior at all, but you do.

People always believe that every thought or action they take will be beneficial to them. No one does anything they think will be bad for themselves. They feel that whatever they're going to do is going to help them, even when experience or logic shows otherwise.

Students always tell me that they wish they had more confidence and that they believed in themselves in a bigger way. The truth, however, is that their negative thinking keeps them safe and so they hang on to their dis-empowering thoughts and actions. They may say they want to have a more positive outlook or belief, but they don't take the action they need to make this so. Why? What could possibly be good about not believing in yourself? You think that if you don't believe in your dreams then you're not going to get hurt, disappointed or feel any kind of pain, but you are totally mistaken.

All negative habits are choices that people make. Choices, which they think, will keep them protected from pain. You must know that no one is born with negative thoughts. They are something you acquire

119

or were given to you. Every unhelpful habit you have is something you have consciously or unconsciously chosen to keep.

If you take drugs or drink excessively, for example, you may not perceive that as destructive behavior. You use drugs or alcohol to escape your life momentarily, to forget your current situation. They may give you the freedom to do some things you would not do in a sober state. So, you see drugs and alcohol as beneficial. You justify any actions by telling yourself that what you're doing is the right thing at that particular time. What can be good about living in pain or sadness? Well... It can get you attention. In life we all strive for attention. There is nothing wrong with that. But if we can't get attention in a positive way we will try to get in a negative way.

Why do you continue with your negative habits? You do it, because you haven't given yourself a good enough reason not to do so. These habits are a protection mechanism that you have created, keeping you from being vulnerable in a world that frightens you. By creating negative habits you think you are guarding yourself against suffering. But these unconstructive behaviors actually hurt you more. So you actually end up with more pain, which you have been so desperately trying to avoid. Crazy, no?

The key to removing your negative habits is to make peace with vulnerability. *The opposite of negativity is vulnerability.* To be vulnerable is to be open, to take risks. If you want all the possibility and excitement that life has to offer you must expose your heart. There is no other way. Yes, you run the risk of feeling pain, but you might also experience great joy and love. It is only in this state that you can achieve your dreams and goals.

"Out of your vulnerabilities will come your strength."
—Freud

Loving someone unconditionally is an act of faith; because you don't know what the other person is going to do or how the other person is going to react. But you must open yourself up in this way if you want to experience love. If you shut yourself off and follow your negative thoughts you are not living life. You simply exist and thus end up living more of a nightmare than the dream that was possible for you.

When you first recognized your dreams you wondered if they would actually come true. You started to ask yourself how realistic these dreams were and your mind began giving you all the negative things that might stand in your way. So you stopped yourself before you even began, holding back from your life's purpose. Now you aren't doing what you were born to do and therefore will never be happy.

Let's talk about the 20% - 80% pain rule. You must recognize that pain is a part of life. By trying to avoid pain you are also closing yourself off to the good things that life has to offer. Sometimes you have to embrace the message of the pain, because it is telling you that you must change something in your life. Let's say that you see someone at a party with whom you would like to speak, but you are afraid to approach that person because he or she might reject you. So you stay put and hold back. You think you are keeping yourself from being hurt, but in actuality you have avoided an opportunity that could have been beneficial to you. The truth is that you might be rejected, which would be about 20% painful. But by not trying to connect with that person you

121

are now filled with regret that can last a lifetime, which is 80% painful. What do you think is the better choice 20% or 80%?

"You suffer forever for all the actions in life you did not take."

How can you get rid of your negative habits?

Write your negative habits away.

Take two minutes and put your negative thoughts on paper. Every sentence must start with "I wish". For example: "I wish I was more open", or "I wish I trusted myself", or "I wish I wasn't so afraid". Then rewrite them in an affirmative manner. For example: "I like not being open", or "I like not trusting myself", or "I like being afraid". Once you do that, you will need to find how these negative thoughts have benefited you. (Trust me you will find it).

Find the benefit of positive behavior.

What's the benefit of being more open? You will welcome more opportunities into your life. It is important to note that only seeing stronger benefits of this new way of thinking will move you toward a new behavior.

Do something unusual.

You have to speak to your negative habits and say, "Thank you for keeping me safe, but I have discovered a new way." Embrace all your pessimistic thoughts with gratitude, knowing that it is time for you to now move on. But those negative thoughts and behaviors will not just leave quietly. They will wait patiently for the right moment to come back into your life, knowing how easy it is to revert to your old habits. So, as you start living a new way, stay vigilant. Those negative thoughts are lurking around the corner...Waiting.

Start living the new habit.

Start taking risks with new positive habits and you will find your road to success. All new habits feel a bit strange at first, but over time they will become second nature to you. Only then can you really begin to realize your dreams. Remember, negative habits will always bring you pain and positive habits can bring you joy. It's your choice.

"The opposite of negativity is vulnerability.

"When Bernie met me he probably thought he was being punished! I was referred to him by a famous Hollywood director I worked with in Australia. I came over to LA to network and begin my "Hollywood invasion"; I'd been searching for a mentor my entire life. I knew from the moment I met him that I had found my mentor. It wasn't just about my acting; it was about ME as a human being.

Prior to meeting Bernard, my acting career was truly on hold. As a child and teenager I worked A LOT on TV and in Theatre. I was on my way to the top! But once I got truly LOST in my head, it all stopped. I was completely out of touch with everyone and everything.

I worked with him full time for 3 weeks. They were the hardest 3 weeks of my life. BUT I KNEW this was right, and I knew, if he couldn't help me, I had no chance.

I dyed my hair back to its original color. I started wearing dresses and found the feminine side of me and began to find my inner child too. It wasn't easy! One year later… I don't even know who that girl was that met him. I am ME again.

I had done everything possible to NOT deal with MY TRUTH. Bernard gave me the gift of life. I truly believe that. I carry it

with me every day, the legacy of what he has taught me. The values he has instilled in me. I respect Bernard Hiller with such magnitude it hurts my heart sometimes."

—**Clementine Heath**
Australian Actress

Israeli and Palestinian actors hugging each other at the
Peres Peace Center in Tel Aviv during my Masterclass.

WHEN THE STUDENT IS READY A MASTERCLASS WILL APPEAR

But what is a great class? Most people don't even know what a great acting class is, because until you are in an amazing class you wouldn't know what you are looking for. I consider that a great acting class should be three things: fun, motivating and very challenging. The training should move you past your own limitations every time you attend. A great class should also be so exciting, that you never want it to end.

Searching for the right class might be your life long task, because it's hard to find the class that is just right for you. Then again, the class is only as good as you are. Even if you are in an amazing class, but you're not a very good student, the class will appear not very good. I was fortunate enough to find some wonderful classes but I always felt there was something missing in the training. Since I did not find what I was looking for, I ended up creating the class I always wanted. This happened in the year 2000 when I was asked to teach a five-week course in Paris.

It all started when I was in the Samuel French Bookstore in Studio City, California, looking for some new acting scenes to give out to my actors when an actress, Karen Strassman, came up to me and asked me what I did. I told her that I was an acting teacher and she said that when she looked at me, she had a feeling that she needed to work with me. I worked with her for a month and that changed her professional life. (She now lives and works in Los Angeles). She told me that she was living in Paris and that I should teach there, because there was no one teaching my messages of hope, craft and how to succeed as an artist. Of course I said, "Yes." I didn't speak French and some people thought that if you don't speak their language, they will never understand your method. But, I felt that I needed to go. I had a feeling that it would all work out. Since that time I have been fortunate enough to consistently teach hundreds of Masterclasses throughout fourteen countries. I feel lucky to be teaching actors in such amazing places.

The teaching experience that changed me the most happened in Rome. This was the first place after the Paris class in which I started to further develop my Masterclass techniques and exercises. The Italian actors I met there were so open and willing to try anything. They really challenged me to make my Masterclass even more powerful, because the greatest reward for me is to see students become the actors they always wanted to be. I realized that I needed to further create an experience that not only explored the techniques of acting, but also explored the human condition and life issues that were holding people back from living their dreams. So I started to create exercises that helped them discover what they were born to do. To break away all of the blocks and fears that were stopping them from becoming fully available and emotionally alive actors, by shutting off their brain and getting them in touch with their heart and instinct. The more you discover of yourself the more you can use. Because of my incredible friend and actress, Suzanna Ruedeberg, who organized my classes in Rome, I started to teach in France, Spain, England and many other countries all over the world. I am very proud to say that I have many success stories based on these classes. They have transformed and changed the lives of the artists I work with and it also changed me. My life has been enriched by working with some of the best artists, casting directors, writers, producers, and directors from all over the world. I always felt that I had one of the best jobs in the world and now I knew that it was true.

There have been so many moments in my classes that transformed me, because I witnessed the power of change and awakening. (Remember, I can only take you to the door of learning. You have to walk through that door to see where my teachings can take you.) One moment in particular brings chills to me whenever I think about it. I was doing an exercise in which the actors had to perform a sexy dance in front of the class as a way to overcome one of their fears and a wonderful African American actor and performer, who was living in Rome was dancing but kept saying, "I can't do this, I can't do this". He was so afraid of looking bad. Everyone in the class was trying to cheer him on, but he just kept saying, "I can't do it", running away from his power and an incredible opportunity for change. I walked up to him and said, "Look I have a dream for you. I have a dream that you can do it". Spontaneously and without warning he started to go into Martin Luther King Jr.'s "I have a dream" speech. In that moment all his passion and thirst for life came pouring out of him and it transformed the entire class. What I didn't know was that he had toured throughout Europe as Martin Luther King Jr. in a one-man show. Once he heard that line he understood that everyone had fears, but that dreams are worth fighting for. No one in that class will ever forget that life changing moment and neither will he. He allowed himself to let go and be ready for the change he needed in his life.

When you think about it, everything you have right now, started as a dream. So cherish your dreams because that's what you were born to do. My dreams are continuing to grow in profound ways. Remember; be ready, grateful and open for the moments that can help you discover the path to your dreams. It will bring you joy, contentment and eventually success. And isn't that what life is all about?

Focusing on my French actors in Paris accompanied by assistant & actor-Jean Christophe Lucchesi.

BECOMING A STAR IS EASY

Some people come into Show-Business for all the wrong reasons. They are unhappy and feel that they have been insignificant all their lives. They come because they would like to be "famous". Because of their need for attention and not having been heard or seen in the past, they feel that acting would be the best way to accomplish visibility and get approval from others. That will of course not work! You must change your mindset to be successful in this profession; otherwise you're dependent on others for your self-worth and happiness. Only by discovering your personal powers you can make your dreams come true.

IT'S IMPORTANT TO LIVE A FULL LIFE

Some students come to my classes without positive relationships or experiencing any real joy in their lives. I have found that unhappy people make lousy students and therefore lousy actors, because they are not living fulfilling lives. They come into acting as a way of experiencing life, but acting is just a copy. It's not the "real thing". You must first live and know the real thing before you can bring anything significant to your acting.

Sometimes people think, "Oh, I am a strange, lonely person, I have gone through a lot of pain and suffering and that is going to make me a good actor." No! Wrong! Suffering a lot and going through a lot of pain just makes you a painful actor. People didn't come to see you suffer, but to bring them understanding, hope and joy. This can only be done once you have found the lesson in your own experiences.

Contrary to popular belief, acting is a joyous profession. The more love and joy that you have the more success you will achieve. You will also be able to bring those feelings to your audience. For you cannot give us, what you do not have. You have to realize that you may have come to acting for the wrong reasons, but you have to quickly understand that Show-Business will not be the parents that you've never had. Show-Business will not give you the love that you were always missing as a child, because it's even more critical and judgmental. If you would like to succeed in this business, you will first have to become a star in your own life.

How do you become a star? You start to live your life like a star. That's right, you think like a star, behave like a star, and react to situations like a star. Stars listen to their instinct and their heart. How will you know when you've become a star in your life? When everyone you know, wants to be like you. You inspire people by your actions and authenticity. They are impressed with how energetic and positive you are, and how you seem to find the joy and excitement of life no matter what is going on. They are amazed at how you overcome your obstacles. If you're not living like this now, you have a lot of work to do.

What most stars have in common is that when they walk into a room they spread joy everywhere they go. They make a difference. They're in meaningful relationships and are experiencing the adventures of life.

I have found that when you've become a star in your own life, you will be able to become a star in your career. (You will need training to make this happen).

The stars that I have worked with always have something special. Acting just saw what they were displaying in life. So, be grateful, optimistic and make the changes you need for a better tomorrow. Understand that acting is a truly rewarding and glorious profession once you come for the right reasons.

"We are all born with limitless potential, so start living like a star now."

"I have been in the People development business for over 22 years and have trained with some of the world's leading figures in Success Coaching. My first Masterclass with Bernard was literally an exhilarating life changing experience, precisely because he is everything that he teaches - the real deal! Since that first class, I have continuously worked with this great teacher in many countries throughout the world and each Masterclass has been a unique magical event."

Some say that Gratitude is the memory of the Heart, I say my Heart always remembers you my friend! Thank you!"

—**Lefteris Samaras**
Greek – Actor

**The amazing Director Garry Marshall thrilled my LA actors.
"Pretty Woman", "Valentine's Day".**

HOW TO MAKE IT IN HOLLYWOOD

I t is the dream that filmmakers and actors from the worldwide artistic and entertainment community, have been thinking about for the last hundred years.

What does Hollywood represent? The BEST! The pinnacle of success and some of the greatest films ever made. Everyday some of the best actors from all over the world come to Hollywood with hopes to succeed. Hollywood is the Mecca. Eighty-five percent of all movies and television shows originate in Hollywood. If you really want to succeed big, Hollywood is where you have to be!

But, it turns out that most people who come here don't succeed. Why is that? The reason is because they don't know the Rules Of Hollywood. I can tell you now that whatever you might think Hollywood is, most don't have a clue, because what you've read in the gossip columns and what people have told you is just not true.

Don't take advice from anyone unless you know they have actually been *successful* in Hollywood. Then they will be able to give you insights into the inner workings and true dynamics of Hollywood and what you might need to do to become successful yourself.

There are many advice books available that will give you information about how to get an agent, market yourself, the websites you need to go to for auditions and the right casting workshops. Those things are important, but they fail to tell you the most important aspects of the business and the reason why only 8% of those who come to Hollywood make it.

Here are The Rules Of Hollywood, which you need to follow to get onto the path of your success.

"The rules are not secret; they are just a secret from you."

THE RULES OF HOLLYWOOD

HOLLYWOOD RULE - ONE.

When you come to Hollywood you have to think, "What am I going to give", not "What am I going to get". Most people come to "get" things they just want something for themselves. Hollywood will not respond to you unless you are ready to give something. That needy energy of wanting to get can be seen in an instant by the people in this industry. Trust me they see it. The more you are willing to give to the people you meet, the more excited and interested they will be in you.

HOLLYWOOD RULE - TWO.

Hollywood runs on energy. If you don't have a great positive energy that is radiating out of your body, you will be unemployed because energy is the Hollywood currency. I find that the people that I have met here who are successful are mostly very nice, caring and happy. George Clooney once said, "I wouldn't want to work with anyone who I couldn't have dinner with".

Hollywood is like a dinner party. Would anyone want to spend six months on set with an unhappy, depressed person? The whole depressed and misunderstood artist thing, just doesn't work. People who are open to their creativity will attract more of those people into their lives. Be open, positive and giving. That type of energy will attract the right people. This leads us to the next rule.

"We don't live in the world, we live in the world we create."

HOLLYWOOD RULE - THREE.

In Hollywood, you don't attract the people you want, you attract who you are. So, if you are a superficial person then you're going to come to Hollywood and meet a lot of superficial people. Users will meet users and sad people meet sad people. In life you always meet the kind of person that you are. If you have negative friends, well that's because you're negative; like attracts like.

I am fully aware that there is a different side of Hollywood as well. A sleazy, dark side. If you encounter these kinds of people then ask yourself, why you are meeting people like that? See what changes you need to make in yourself to attract the people you want. Because you don't live in the world, you live in the world you create.

The world I have worked to create for myself includes artists who are making a difference in life. As artists we have the opportunity and ability to do that.

HOLLYWOOD RULE - FOUR.

Be Pro-active, not re-active. Hollywood admires people who don't sit around and complain or blame anyone. What Hollywood likes is for artists to take their own careers back into their control. Let me say that again. What Hollywood likes are artists who take control of their own destiny. They like people who make their own films, create their own projects. The business has changed, now you can make your own film with the current technology. It is not enough to just be an actor looking for a job. A true artist does not need to be told to create; they are always in motion.

Hollywood is also open to recognizing artists who are not from the United States. There is no other city that is so open to foreigners. In Hollywood anyone who is nominated from any country could win. This is the only city I know where dreams can come true. Where else would you have an Arnold Schwarzenegger, who came here barely speaking English, but with a drive to succeed in becoming a super-star? What he did have was discipline and an amazing work ethic. He told me that he had clear goals and felt unstoppable. Clearly his ambitions and hard work paid off.

HOLLYWOOD RULE - FIVE.

Gratitude. One of the things that Hollywood likes very much is gratitude. It likes you to appreciate people for their efforts. I have noticed that the big stars always thank people for helping them. I find that most of the people at the top are thoughtful of others. They tell me that they feel fortunate that they have a job. They tell me that they feel grateful to be in this business. Some realize that it is not just about being a "movie star", but how can they use that found fame to help benefit the world. I am very proud to come from an industry that is making such a difference. A lot of these stars use their notoriety for charities, but as George Clooney once told me, when I asked him why he gets involved with so many causes around the world, "It's a chip that I can use right now, I can make a difference and I will take it."

Hollywood raises enormous amounts of money for causes and charities all over the world.

HOLLYWOOD RULE - SIX.

Connect to people. You have to do something that my acting teacher told me long ago, you have to learn how to connect and get along with people. You have to learn how to turn people on with your humanity so that they will want to work with you. You have to realize that you have to learn how to build bridges. It's easy to build a wall, but it's hard to build a bridge. Go to screenings, attend seminars, get involved in causes and just get out there. You never know who you are going to meet.

HOLLYWOOD RULE - SEVEN.

Ask for help. You can't do anything alone. You need help from a strong artistic community, a mentor or people that are working towards your same goals. Don't ask for help from unmotivated friends who really know nothing about what is going on in this industry. Everything I have learned I learnt from someone kind enough to share their information with me. It doesn't belittle your accomplishments. Nothing can be done alone. If you are genuine you should be meeting people that will want to help you and in turn, you will help them. It's when *you* start helping people that miracles will occur.

Hollywood is known as a small community. To achieve anything great here, you have to have a lot of collaborators. There are over a hundred people involved in making a film. You couldn't make a film on your own. In fact, the only thing you can do alone is fail. In order to create something you will need to inspire others. So have a personality where other people want to be with you. You must be able to inspire and articulate your vision. Remember everyone wants to be involved in a project that has meaning.

(᠕⊶)

"You never know how far you can go until you go as far as you can go."

SUMMARY

Life is created out of the choices you make. The way you make it in Hollywood is that you have to have enormous energy, openness, gratitude, a sense of giving and a meaningful dream full of passion. Ask for help and be thankful for what you have and where you are in your journey. Hollywood is the only place on the planet that everyone wants to know what's going on here.

They admire it because they are surprised and shocked by it. It gives so much to the international community. I can tell you that if you are ever serious about becoming an artist in the film industry, you must come here at least once, to see what's going on. It doesn't mean you have to stay, but you have to come here, because the best of the very best come here to study, create and grow. Hollywood is the Olympics for acting. Or as I like to say, it's the Olympics for the Olympics. The best of the very best of all the industry are here. Come join me if you think you have what it takes. A lot of work will need to be done. Because, *the express elevator to success is broken, so you will have to take the stairs.* But, what's beautiful about that is, if you can make it here, you can make it anywhere.

"Remember: The bigger the dream the better the life."

—Bernard Hiller

The Academy Awards
See you here next year!
Love, Bernard Hiller
Beverly Hills, California

www.bernardhiller.com

Acknowledgements

There are people you meet for a reason, for a season or for a lifetime. These people mentioned below are people that I'll have to thank for a lifetime for all they have done for me. I will never forget all your love, insight, knowledge and support that you have given me. Without you, this work and this book would never have happened.

Susanna Laura Ruedeberg, Lefteris Samaras, Sandra De Sousa, Jean Christophe Lucchesi, Federica Picone, Sarah Schultz, Rudy Gentile, John Philip Law, Adrian Gaeta, Brett Ratner, Karen Strassman, Lisa Taback, Kasia Nabialczyk, Barry Navidi, Sheila Rubin, Kate Nichols, Nadia Tumas, Bernd Capitain, April Webster and special thanks to the amazing songstress Eva Cassidy.

Of course I would not be anywhere without the support of my extended artistic family here in Los Angeles and in the different countries that I have taught.

I want to also thank the acting profession and my instincts for telling me what to do next. Through this glorious profession I've been lucky enough to meet such amazing human beings all over the world. I will be forever grateful.

STOP ACTING START LIVING

~TELE-SEMINARS~

JOIN AN EXCLUSIVE GROUP OF ARTISTS AND TRAIN WITH BERNARD HILLER

**Send an email with your contact information
and the code BKGROUPS8 in the subject line to**

StopActingStartLiving@gmail.com

~

REMEMBER:
THE BIGGER THE DREAM
THE BETTER THE LIFE

CPSIA information can be obtained
at www.ICGtesting.com
Printed in the USA
FSOW04n1619040816
23424FS